# First World War
### and Army of Occupation
# War Diary
### France, Belgium and Germany

34 DIVISION
102 Infantry Brigade
Headquarters
1 July 1918 - 31 August 1918

WO95/2461/3

The Naval & Military Press Ltd
www.nmarchive.com
**Published in association with The National Archives**

Published by

The Naval & Military Press Ltd

Unit 10 Ridgewood Industrial Park,
Uckfield, East Sussex,
TN22 5QE England
Tel: +44 (0) 1825 749494

www.naval-military-press.com
www.nmarchive.com

*This diary has been reprinted in facsimile from the original. Any imperfections are inevitably reproduced and the quality may fall short of modern type and cartographic standards.*

© **Crown Copyright**
**Images reproduced by permission of The National Archives, London, England, 2015.**

# Contents

| Document type | Place/Title | Date From | Date To |
|---|---|---|---|
| Heading | War Diary & Appendices July-1918 Headquarters-102nd Inf. Brigade Vol XXXII. Vol 31 | | |
| War Diary | Oost Cappel. | 01/07/1918 | 06/07/1918 |
| War Diary | School Camp. | 07/07/1918 | 13/07/1918 |
| War Diary | Cormette Camp. | 14/07/1918 | 15/07/1918 |
| War Diary | Oost. Cappel. | 16/07/1918 | 17/07/1918 |
| War Diary | Rexpoede. | 17/07/1918 | 17/07/1918 |
| War Diary | Borest. | 18/07/1918 | 19/07/1918 |
| War Diary | Vez. | 20/07/1918 | 20/07/1918 |
| War Diary | Puiseux. | 21/07/1918 | 22/07/1918 |
| War Diary | Montramboeuf Farm. | 23/07/1918 | 28/07/1918 |
| War Diary | Bois De La Baillette. | 29/07/1918 | 31/07/1918 |
| Operation(al) Order(s) | 102nd Infantry Brigade Order No. 219 App.1 (A). | 08/07/1918 | 08/07/1918 |
| Miscellaneous | March Table-To accompany 102nd Inf. Bde. Order No. 219. | | |
| Miscellaneous | 102nd Infantry Brigade Exercise No. 1. App 2 (A). | 09/07/1918 | 09/07/1918 |
| Miscellaneous | To accompany 102nd Inf. Bde. Exercise No. 1. Instructions regarding 102nd Inf. Bde. Exercise No. 1. | 09/07/1918 | 09/07/1918 |
| Miscellaneous | T.S. 36/12 Reference Maps Sheets 27 N.E. & 28 N.W.1/20,000. | 06/07/1918 | 06/07/1918 |
| Operation(al) Order(s) | 102nd Infantry Brigade Order No. 220. App 1 (B). | 11/07/1918 | 11/07/1918 |
| Operation(al) Order(s) | 102nd Infantry Brigade Order No. 221. App 1 C. | 12/07/1918 | 12/07/1918 |
| Miscellaneous | Table "A"-To accompany 102nd Inf. Bde. Order No. 221.Starting Point. Entrance to School Camp on main Poperinghe Watou Road., L.3.a.8.4. | | |
| Miscellaneous | Table "B"-To accompany 102nd Inf. Bde. Order No. 221.Starting Point-Road Junction, St Jans ter Biezen-L.2.a.5.7. | | |
| Operation(al) Order(s) | Administrative Instructions issued with 102nd Brigade Order No. 221. | 12/07/1918 | 12/07/1918 |
| Operation(al) Order(s) | 102nd Infantry Brigade Order No. 222. App ID. | 14/07/1918 | 14/07/1918 |
| Miscellaneous | | | |
| Miscellaneous | Table "A"-To accompany 102nd Inf. Bde. Order No. 222. Starting-Point Cross Roads 400" East of last E in Cormette. | | |
| Operation(al) Order(s) | Addendum No. 1. 102nd Infantry Brigade Order No. 223. App I E. | 15/07/1918 | 15/07/1918 |
| Operation(al) Order(s) | 102nd Infantry Brigade Order No. 223. | 15/07/1918 | 15/07/1918 |
| Miscellaneous | Table "A"-To accompany 102nd Inf. Bde. Order No. 223. Starting Point-Cross Roads 400 East of last E in Cormette. | 15/07/1918 | 15/07/1918 |
| Operation(al) Order(s) | 102nd Infantry Brigade Order No. 223. App I. E. | 15/07/1918 | 15/07/1918 |
| Miscellaneous | Table "A"-To accompany 102nd Inf. Bde. Order No. 223. Starting Point-Cross Roads 400 East of last E in Cormette. | 15/07/1918 | 15/07/1918 |
| Operation(al) Order(s) | 102nd Infantry Brigade Order No. 224. App I F. | 15/07/1918 | 15/07/1918 |
| Operation(al) Order(s) | 102nd Infantry Brigade Order No. 215. Appendix No. 1 (c). | 15/06/1918 | 15/06/1918 |
| Miscellaneous | 102nd Brigade Administrative Instructions No. 2. | 15/07/1918 | 15/07/1918 |
| Miscellaneous | 102nd Infantry Brigade No. 225. App I G. | 19/07/1918 | 19/07/1918 |

| Type | Description | Date | Date |
|---|---|---|---|
| Operation(al) Order(s) | 102nd Bde. Order No. 225. | 20/07/1918 | 20/07/1918 |
| Operation(al) Order(s) | 102nd Infantry Brigade Order No. 226. App I A. | 20/07/1918 | 20/07/1918 |
| Operation(al) Order(s) | 102nd Infantry Brigade Order No. 227 App II. | 21/07/1918 | 21/07/1918 |
| Miscellaneous | March Table-To accompany 102nd Inf. Bde. Order No. 227. | | |
| Operation(al) Order(s) | 102nd Infantry Brigade Order No. 228 App I J. | 23/07/1918 | 23/07/1918 |
| Miscellaneous | Plan Of Attack. | | |
| Miscellaneous | Table "A"-To accompany 102nd Infantry Brigade Order No. 224. | | |
| Operation(al) Order(s) | 102 Infantry Brigade Order No. 229. App I K. | 27/07/1918 | 27/07/1918 |
| Operation(al) Order(s) | 102nd Infantry Brigade Order No 230. | 31/07/1918 | 31/07/1918 |
| Miscellaneous | To O.C. 2/4 Somersets | 31/07/1918 | 31/07/1918 |
| Miscellaneous | To O.C. 1/4 Cheshire. | 31/07/1918 | 31/07/1918 |
| Operation(al) Order(s) | 102nd Infantry Brigade Order No. 230. App I Z. | 28/07/1918 | 28/07/1918 |
| Miscellaneous | To accompany 102nd Inf. Bde. Order No. 230. Starting Point-X Roads-5906 (Point 132)-(Oulcry Le Chateau). | | |
| Operation(al) Order(s) | 102nd Infantry Brigade Order No. 231. App 1 11. | 31/07/1918 | 31/07/1918 |
| Miscellaneous | Cover for Documents. Nature of Enclosures. | | |
| Heading | War Diary 102nd Infantry Brigade H.Q. August 1918 Volume XXXIII Vol 32 | | |
| War Diary | Palis Line. | 01/08/1918 | 03/08/1918 |
| War Diary | Silly Le-Long. | 03/08/1918 | 05/08/1918 |
| War Diary | Zeggers Cappel. | 06/08/1918 | 12/08/1918 |
| War Diary | Herzeele. | 13/08/1918 | 18/08/1918 |
| War Diary | Proven. | 19/08/1918 | 27/08/1918 |
| War Diary | Cormette. | 27/08/1918 | 31/08/1918 |
| Heading | Appendices For War Diary 102nd Infantry Brigade H.Q. August-1918 Volume XXXIII. | | |
| Operation(al) Order(s) | Infantry Brigade Order No. 239. App I A. | 02/08/1918 | 02/08/1918 |
| Operation(al) Order(s) | 102nd Infantry Brigade Order No. 232. App I A. | 03/08/1918 | 03/08/1918 |
| Miscellaneous | Table "A"-To accompany 102nd Infantry Brigade Order No. 232. Starting Point-Point Where Paris line Cuts Beugneux-Oulchy-Le-Chateau Road. | | |
| Miscellaneous | Table "B"-To accompany 102nd Inf. Brigade Order No. 232. Starting Point-Road Junction Just W. of Oulchy Le Ville. | | |
| Miscellaneous | Table "C"-To accompany 102nd Inf. Bde Order No. 232. Starting Point-As selected by off. i/c 102nd Bde. Group. | | |
| Miscellaneous | 102nd Brigade Administrative Instructions No. 208 | 03/08/1918 | 03/08/1918 |
| Operation(al) Order(s) | Addendum to 102nd Infantry Brigade Order No. 232. App I. | 05/08/1918 | 05/08/1918 |
| Miscellaneous | 102nd Infantry Bde. Addendum No. 1. to Defence Scheme-Reserve Brigade-34th Div. App 2 A. | 24/08/1918 | 24/08/1918 |
| Miscellaneous | Defence Scheme. Reserve Brigade-34th Division. | | |
| Operation(al) Order(s) | Addendum to 102nd Infantry Brigade Order No. 303. | 05/08/1918 | 05/08/1918 |
| Miscellaneous | Table "D". Entraining Table to accompany 102nd Inf. Bde. Order No. 303 (Addendum). Entraining Station Le Plessis Belleville. | | |
| Miscellaneous | 102nd Infantry Brigade Administrative Instructions. No. 6. | 08/08/1918 | 08/08/1918 |
| Operation(al) Order(s) | 102nd Brigade Administrative Instructions No. 6. | 05/08/1918 | 05/08/1918 |
| Operation(al) Order(s) | 102nd Infantry Brigade Order No. 233. App I B. | 12/08/1918 | 12/08/1918 |
| Miscellaneous | Table "A"-To accompany 102nd Infantry Brigade Order No. 233. | | |

| Type | Description | Date | Date |
|---|---|---|---|
| Miscellaneous | Amendment No. 1 To 102nd Infantry Brigade Order No. 234. App I C. | | |
| Operation(al) Order(s) | 102nd Infantry Brigade Order No. 234. | 18/08/1918 | 18/08/1918 |
| Miscellaneous | March Table "A"-To accompany 102nd Infantry Brigade Order No. 234. Starting Point-Cross Roads 500 X East of Herzeele D.10.d.1.6. | | |
| Miscellaneous | Table "B" to accompany 102nd Inf. Bde.Order No. 234 (Add. No. 3-Amendt. No. 1) Starting Point. Cross Roads F.21.a.2.6. (Sheet 27). | | |
| Operation(al) Order(s) | Addendum No. 2 to 102nd Infantry Brigade Order No & 234. | 19/08/1918 | 19/08/1918 |
| Operation(al) Order(s) | Addendum No. 1 to 102nd Infantry Brigade Order No. 234. | 18/08/1918 | 18/08/1918 |
| Miscellaneous | Amendment to 102nd Brigade Administrative Instructions No. 9. | 18/08/1918 | 18/08/1918 |
| Miscellaneous | 102nd Brigade Administrative Instructions No. 9. | 18/08/1918 | 18/08/1918 |
| Miscellaneous | Provisional Defence Scheme. Reserve Brigade. | 21/08/1918 | 21/08/1918 |
| Operation(al) Order(s) | Addendum No. 2 to 102nd Infantry Brigade Order No& 234. | 19/08/1918 | 19/08/1918 |
| Operation(al) Order(s) | 102nd Infantry Brigade Order No. 235. App I D. | | |
| Operation(al) Order(s) | 102nd Infantry Brigade Order No. 235. | | |
| Miscellaneous | Addendum No. 3 to 102nd Infantry Brigade Order No. 234. | 20/08/1918 | 20/08/1918 |
| Miscellaneous | 102nd Infantry Brigade Administrative Instructions No. 10. to accompany 102nd Brigade Order No. 234 Addendum No. 3. | 20/08/1918 | 20/08/1918 |
| Miscellaneous | T.S. 35/9. | 25/08/1918 | 25/08/1918 |
| Miscellaneous | 34th Division. Defence Instructions No. 4. Demolition. | 23/08/1918 | 23/08/1918 |
| Miscellaneous | List "A"-Forward Group. | | |
| Miscellaneous | Battalion Signal Officer. | | |
| Operation(al) Order(s) | 102nd Infantry Brigade Order No. 236. App I E. | 26/08/1918 | 26/08/1918 |
| Miscellaneous | 102nd Infantry Brigade Administrative Instructions No. 11. To accompany 102nd Brigade Order No. 236-August 26th, 1918. | 26/08/1918 | 26/08/1918 |
| Miscellaneous | 102nd Infantry Brigade Administrative Instructions No. 12. To accompany 102nd Brigade Order No. 237 dated 27/8/18. | 27/08/1918 | 27/08/1918 |
| Miscellaneous | Table "A" (To accompany 102nd Inf. Bde. Order No. 236). | | |
| Miscellaneous | Table "B" (To accompany 102nd Inf. Bde. Order No. 233 Starting Point. Cross Roads 28/A.23.a.9.0. | | |
| Miscellaneous | II, Corps G.S. 9. | 27/08/1918 | 27/08/1918 |
| Operation(al) Order(s) | 102nd Infantry Brigade Order No. 237. App IF. | 27/08/1918 | 27/08/1918 |
| Operation(al) Order(s) | 102nd Infantry Brigade Order No. 237. | 27/08/1918 | 27/08/1918 |
| Miscellaneous | March Table "A"-To accompany Bde. Order No. 237. | | |
| Miscellaneous | March Table "B"-To accompany 102nd Inf. Bde. Order No. 237. | | |
| Miscellaneous | Table "D". Entraining Table to accompany 102nd Inf. Bde. Order No. 232. (Addendum). Entraining Station Le Plessis Belleville. | | |

Vol 31

Volume XXXII.

# War Diary
# & Appendices

July – 1918

Headquarters – 102nd Inf. Brigade

12.8.1918

*Edward Hilliam*

Brigadier General.
Commdg. 102 Inf. Brigade

# WAR DIARY
## INTELLIGENCE SUMMARY.

Army Form C. 2118.

REFCE MAPS 8/M 5776 19+27 1/40,000

| Place | Date | Hour | Summary of Events and Information | Remarks and references to Appendices |
|---|---|---|---|---|
| OOST CAPPEL | July 1st | — | New Units (101st Infantry Brigade arrived in BAMBECQUE AREA (units from 53rd Division from PALESTINE came under orders of G O C 102nd Inf Bde as follows. 1/4th Bn CHES REGT – 1/7th Bn CHES R – 1/11th Bn HEREFORDS REGT. Transport which had proceeded in advance moved from BAMBR AREA & joined units in BAMBECQUE AREA. | |
| — " — | July 2nd & 3rd | — | Training & organization of Battalions carried out under Battalions arrangements | |
| — " — | July 4th | — | Inspection of Battalions by G.O.C. 34th Division | |
| — " — | July 5th | — | Training continued | |
| — " — | July 6th | — | 102nd Inf Bde ordered to move to SCHOOL CAMP just E. of ST JANSTER BIEZEN Bde order No 219 issued ordering move of Brigade | App (A) |
| SCHOOL CAMP | July 7th | — | 102nd Inf Bde moved by March route via HOUTKERQUE – WATOU to SCHOOL CAMP arriving at 12 noon | |
| — " — | July 8th | — | Training at SCHOOL CAMP commenced | |
| — " — | July 9th | — | Second Army Commander inspected the 102nd Inf/Aux Inf Brigade (Bns training) on parade ground at SCHOOL CAMP | |

# WAR DIARY
## INTELLIGENCE SUMMARY

Army Form C. 2118.

REFCE. MAPS. SHEETS 27 1/9 1/40,000
HAZEBROUCK 1/100,000

| Place | Date | Hour | Summary of Events and Information | Remarks and references to Appendices |
|---|---|---|---|---|
| SCHOOL CAMP | July 9th | — | At dark the 102nd Inf. Brigade carried out practice occupation of the right sector of the EAST POPERINGHE LINE in accordance with 102 Inf. Bde Exercise No 1. arriving back in camp by 2.30 A.M | APP.2.(A) |
| " | July 10th | — | Training Continued. Battalions left Camp for Gas Chamber. 102nd L.T.M.B. formed by drafts from Base & other Divisions. | APP.(3) |
| " | July 11th | — | As for 10th. Brigade Order No 220 issued re. Right Sec (A) of E. POPERINGHE LINE | |
| " | July 12th | — | Wet weather interfered with training. 102nd Inf Bde Order No 221 issued re a move of Brigade to COMIETTE MUSKETRY CAMP | |
| " | July 13th | — | 102nd Inf. Brigade instead of PROVEN Stn drawn moving on relief by 101st Inf Brigade & entrained at ST OMER Instead marching to COMIETTE MUSKETRY CAMP for five days training. Transport did so but Infantry had own marching same time as indft - ] AT 102nd L.T.M.B. proceeded to I & II Corps School MILLAIN Musketry training Commenced at 9 A.M. — was carried on throughout the day | |
| COMIETTE CAMP | July 14th | — | 102nd Inf. Bde Order No 222 issued refer move of Brigade into Buttens | |

Army Form C. 2118.

# WAR DIARY
## or
## INTELLIGENCE SUMMARY.
*(Erase heading not required.)*

REFCE. MAPS
HAZEBROUCK SH. 1/100,000

| Place | Date | Hour | Summary of Events and Information | Remarks and references to Appendices |
|---|---|---|---|---|
| COMETTE CAMP | July 4th | — | Warning Wire received from 34th Division for Brigade to be ready to move at short notice | |
| " | July 5th | — | 34 Div wire received ordering immediate move of 102nd Inf Bde to Rousbrugge — H road to BAMBECQUE AREA. Transport started off 1 P.M. 102 Inf Bde order No 223 and Addendum issued with reference to move. | (NONE) |
| | | 5.30 P.M | Battalions commenced entraining STOMER STN. | |
| | | 8.30 P.M | Battalions detrained ROUSBRUGGE STN & marched to billets as under:— 1/4th Bn CHES. R. — HOFLAND E. — 1/1 11th Bn CHES R. BAMBECQUE — 1/1st Bn HEREFORD R. OOST CAPPEL — BDE H.Q. OOST CAPPEL 102nd Inf Bde order No 224 issued with reference to move of 102nd Inf Bde to XXII Corps area | |
| OOST CAPPEL | July 6th | 11.30 A.M | 102nd Inf Brigade Group commenced entraining at ARNEKE STATION in accordance with Brigade Order No 224 | |
| — | July 7th | — | 102nd Inf Bde proceeded via BERGUES — DUNKERQUE — CALAIS — BOULOGNE — ETAPLES — ABBEVILLE — EU — AIBANCOURT — PONTOISE — CREIL to CHANTILLY + SURVILLIERS where units detrained. | |

Army Form C. 2118.

# WAR DIARY
## or
## INTELLIGENCE SUMMARY.
(Erase heading not required.)

HAZEBROUCK SH. 1/100,000
BEAUVAIS SH. 1/100,000
SOISSONS SH. 1/100,000

Instructions regarding War Diaries and Intelligence Summaries are contained in F.S. Regs., Part II. and the Staff Manual respectively. Title pages will be prepared in manuscript.

| Place | Date | Hour | Summary of Events and Information | Remarks and references to Appendices |
|---|---|---|---|---|
| RENPOEDE | July 7 | 4.50 P.M | Last unit of 102nd Brigade Group entrained. Brigade located in new area as follows. (Reserve French Army)<br>BDE. H.Q. BOREST – 1/1st BN HEREF R. BOREST – 1/4th BN CHES R. FONTAINE<br>1/7th BN CHES. R. MONTLOGNON | |
| BOREST. | July 8th | — | Units rested. | |
|  |  | 2.P.M. | Last unit of Brigade Group detrained. | |
|  |  | 10 P.M | Orders received for Brigade to be ready to move in early morning of 9th. Brigade Major proceeded to Senous to receive verbal instruction. | |
| — " — | July 9 | — | 102nd Infy Brigade Order No 225 issued.<br>6 A.M Units commenced entraining in French Lorries – Completed 7.30. A.M<br>Buses proceeded via SENLIS – CREPY EN VALOIS to VAUCIENNES when Brigade debussed & marched to billets as follows arriving 3 A.M:–<br>BDE. H.Q. VEZ. 1/4th BN CHES R. VEZ B.C.H.M.G. BN VAUCIENNES<br>1/7th BATTN CHES. R. VEZ 1/1st BN HER. R. VAUMOISE | App¹ (9). |

**Army Form C. 2118.**

# WAR DIARY
## or
## INTELLIGENCE SUMMARY.

SOISSONS 34. 1/100,000
OULCHY LE CHATEAU (Sud) 1/20,000

(Erase heading not required.)

Instructions regarding War Diaries and Intelligence Summaries are contained in F. S. Regs., Part II. and the Staff Manual respectively. Title pages will be prepared in manuscript.

| Place | Date | Hour | Summary of Events and Information | Remarks and references to Appendices |
|---|---|---|---|---|
| VEZ | July 20th | — | 102nd Inf. Bde. Order No 226 issued before move to PUISEUX | APP 1 (H) |
| | | — | 102nd Inf. Bde. started marching 11.20 P.M. Bde. LARGM 6 main body — | |
| | | — | VILLERS COTTERET Rd. as one hour halt was necessary to permit 101st Inf. Bde. to pass. | |
| | | 7 A.M. | March continued via VILLERS COTTERET + FOREST to PUISEUX where whole Bde. was billeted arriving 6 A.M. | |
| PUISEUX | July 21st | | Brigade rested at PUISEUX | |
| PUISEUX | July 22nd | — | 102nd Inf. Brigade warned to be ready to move forward to take over part of the line now held by 38th French Division. | |
| | | | 102nd Inf Bde order No 227 issued, with refs to taking over from the French. | APP 1 (I) |
| | | | Infantry marched via VILLERS-COTTERET—FOREST—LONGPONT & were met by French guides & were conducted to a new area N. of MOULIN DE VILLERS-HELON | |
| | | | Conference of Commanding Officers was held at Bde. H.Q. in wood & orders given for attack the following morning | |
| MONTRAMBOEUF FARM | July 23 | 1.45AM | Relief of French Troops Completed | |
| | | | Dispositions for the attack | |
| | | | 1/7 Bn. Gus. Rs. on right resting on PAREY—TIGNY—COUTREMIAIN Rd Frontpost | |
| | | | 1/1st Bn Herts Rs. on left resting on TIGNY—MONTRAMBOEUF FM Rd Jnc W of BOIS DE REUGNY | |

Army Form C. 2118.

# WAR DIARY
## or
## INTELLIGENCE SUMMARY.
(Erase heading not required.)

Army Form C. 2118. OULAN 17 BN 97390 1/20,000

| Place | Date | Hour | Summary of Events and Information | Remarks and references to Appendices |
|---|---|---|---|---|
| MONTRAP/136 BIS FARM | July 23 | 5 A.M. | Barrage commenced. 101st Inf. Bde. were to attack on the right & the 115th Tirailleurs on the left of road Inf. Bde. to assemble with Brigade green No. 228. | APP. 1 (J) |
| | | 7.20 A.M. | Wire was received from 34th Division that attack of 34th Division was to be launched at 7.40 A.M. though apparently little progress had been made on the left flank. | |
| | | | During early morning reports received from Battalions. (The attack had been held up by M.G. fire from TIGNY & the BOIS DE REUGNY & by unsuccessful endeavours to advance on the flanks. 1/1st Bn. Hereford R. reported having advanced their line 1000 yards & that they were digging in 200 x W. of the BOIS DE REUGNY. The 1/7 Bn. Glos. R. were ordered to bring up their left to conform & to push their right into touch with the 10th Inf. Bde. on the PARIS DEFENCE LINE which lay PERCY-TIGNY-COURTEMAN R). | |
| | | 12.30 P.M. | Information was received that the 58th French Division on the left had been heavily counter attacked & the Brigade was ordered to dig in on the ground won. | |
| | | | Estimated casualties were given as: 1/4th Batt. Glos. R. 3 off. 140 O.R. 1/7th Glos. R. 2 off. 150 O.R. 1/1st Bn. Hereford R. 12 off. 250 O.R. | |

Army Form C. 2118.

# WAR DIARY
## or
## INTELLIGENCE SUMMARY.
(Erase heading not required.)

Instructions regarding War Diaries and Intelligence Summaries are contained in F.S. Regs., Part II. and the Staff Manual respectively. Title pages will be prepared in manuscript.

Refce Maps Soissons 1/100,000
Oulchy-le Chateau 1/20,000

| Place | Date | Hour | Summary of Events and Information | Remarks and references to Appendices |
|---|---|---|---|---|
| MONT RAMBOEUF FARM | July 23 | 6. PM | Orders were issued for a renewal of the attack but these were cancelled later. During the night 1/4 Bn Che. R. relieved 1/4 Bn Here/who R who withdrew to reserve in the PARIS LINE about PARCY TIGNY. During the night four line Battalions were disposed in depth. | |
| " | July 24 | — | Night passed quietly. There was continuous shelling throughout the day, more especially on the front of left Battn. Yellow & Blue Cross Shells were used causing considerable casualties. 1 Wounded German found by 1/4 Bn Che R | |
| " | July 25 | — | Night passed quietly. Patrols did not encounter the enemy Except for intermittent shelling day was quiet | |
| " | July 26 | — | Quiet day & night. | |
| | | 2.45 PM | G.O.C. Division held conference & rreconked probable move further South & attack in conjunction with the French | |
| " | July 27 | — | Representatives from 12th French Division reconnoitred the line 102nd Inf. Bde. Order No 229 issued re relief by French Relief of Units commenced at dark | |

D.D. & L., London, E.C.
(A801) Wt.W17/M2031 759,000 5/17 Sch. 52 Forms C2. 16/14

# WAR DIARY
## INTELLIGENCE SUMMARY

Army Form C. 2118.

**Instructions regarding War Diaries and Intelligence Summaries are contained in F.S. Regs, Part II. and the Staff Manual respectively. Title pages will be prepared in manuscript.**

(Erase heading not required.)

REFCE MAPS.
SOISSONS 1/100,000
OULCHY-LE-CHATEAU 1/20,000

| Place | Date | Hour | Summary of Events and Information | Remarks and references to Appendices |
|---|---|---|---|---|
| MONTRAMBOEUF FARM | July 28th | 2 A.M | Command of Brigade handed to O.C. 350th French Regiment. Units of Brigade marched independently to BOIS-DE-NADON. Bde H.Q. established at FME BELLEVUE. All units in bivouacs by 6 A.M. Units spent day resting. 102nd Inf. Bde. order No 230 issued containing instructions for assembly & attack. Battalions left BOIS DE NADON at 10 P.M. & marched via ST REMY-BLANZY -FME DE FRONTENY to BOIS DE LA BAILLETTE. | APP.1.(4) |
| BOIS DE LA BAILLETTE | July 29 | 2 A.M | 3 Battalions of 102nd Brigade to-gether with fighting portion of transport in position in BOIS DE LA BAILLETTE. Some casualties caused by shelling during assembly. 2 Battalions were in Divisional Reserve. 1/4 7th Bn Cha.R. in N.W. portion of wood were held in Corps Reserve. | |
| | | 4.50 A.M | Attack launched by 101st & 103rd Inf. Bde from positions E. of the BOIS DE LA BAILLETTE. 1/4 7th Bn Cheshire Regt. moved at dawn & at 5 A.M. were in position along VERS-SOISSONS Rd W. of MAUNS CHATEAU-THIERRY-SOISSONS Rd ready to resist any attempt at counter-attacks from its North. 1/7 Bn Cha. R. 1/1st Bn Hereford R. + 2/1st Bn Mon L.I. (Divn Reserve) came under orders of G.O.C. 102nd Inf. Bde. moved forward to positions along VERS-SOISSONS Rd & later to PARIS LINE between GRAND ROZOY & SUICHY-LE-CHATEAU-BEUGNEUX RD. | |
| | | 10. A.M | The attack of the 2 leading Brigades was held up along the line BEUGNEUX-GRAND ROZOY. Renewal of attack by 1/7th Cha.R. & 2/4 Bn L.I. at 2.30 A.M. was unsuccessful owing to the fact that no covering barrage being given to troops to kick up the barrage. | |

Army Form C. 2118.

# WAR DIARY
## or
## INTELLIGENCE SUMMARY.
(Erase heading not required.)

Instructions regarding War Diaries and Intelligence Summaries are contained in F.S. Regs., Part II. and the Staff Manual respectively. Title pages will be prepared in manuscript.

REFCE MAPS
OULCHY-LE-CHATEAU 1/20,000
1/100,000
BUSSNJ

| Place | Date | Hour | Summary of Events and Information | Remarks and references to Appendices |
|---|---|---|---|---|
| BOIS DE LA BAULETTE | July 29 | — | Divisional sector front BEUGNEUX to GRAND ROZOY re-adjusted during the night. 103rd Inf. Bde on right – 102nd Inf. Bde in centre – 101st Inf. Bde on left. Orders issued for a line of posts to be established along BEUGNEUX-GRAND ROZOY Rd. Owing to evacuation of GRAND ROZOY by the French during the night the left flank of the Brigade was being observed. Posts were successfully pushed forward as ordered before dawn. | |
| | July 30 | — | Morning very quiet. Intermittent hostile shelling during remainder of day & throughout the night. | |
| | July 31 | — | Considerable hostile shelling throughout the day, mainly directed against MONTCEAU WOOD area. 102nd Inf. Bde order No 231 issued for a renewal of the attack. During the night Units of 102nd Inf. Bde with exception of line of posts held by 1 Company of 1/1 Bn. Cks. R. withdrew to reserve positions in accordance with Bde. Order No 231. Assembly for attack completed by midnight. | APP. 1 (M) |

CASUALTIES DURING OPERATIONS ON VESLE FRONT, TO JULY 31ST

KILLED. 2 OFF. 19 O.R. WOUNDED 20 OFF. 670 O.R. GASSED 2 OFF 240 O.R.
MISSING. 23 O.R. TOTAL OFFICERS. 24. ORs 959

Ernest Wellham BRIG-GEN.
COMMDG 102ND INF. BRIGADE

SECRET.

APP.1(A)
COPY No.
21

## 102nd INFANTRY BRIGADE ORDER No. 219

Ref. Maps
Sheets 19 & 27
1:40,000.
6th July, 1918.

1. The 102nd Infantry Brigade will move from the BAMBECQUE Area to SCHOOLS CAMP, L.3.c.9.8., to-morrow, the 7th instant in accordance with attached March Table.

2. *Marching in states will be forwarded so as to reach this office by 10.0 p.m. tonight. Watches will be synchronised with watch sent to Units by dr. D.R. tonight.*

   Distances as laid down in 34th Div. G.S. 7/34 dated 30.6.18 forwarded under this office letter T.S. 67/1 dated 2.7.1918, will be observed on the line of march.

   After passing the starting point a 10 minutes halt will be made by units at 10 minutes to each clock hour.

3. The order of march in Battalions will be as follows -

   Battalion Runners.
   Battalion Signallers.
   Band (if any)
   Four Companies.
   M.O. - Stretcher Bearers.
   1 Officer & Regtl. Police, to collect any stragglers who will be marched in rear of Battalions.
   Transport - (one brecksman to march behind - not on the side of - each vehicle).

   Steel helmets will be carried under the straps of the pack.

4. Strictest march discipline will be observed. Units will march on the right of the road. Officers in charge of Units will be responsible for march discipline, keeping of correct distances and touch with units in front.
   All mounted Officers will be mounted.

5.. In accordance with instructions already issued, the following advance parties will proceed to SCHOOLS CAMP on the evening of the 6th inst. to take over billets, training stores and particulars of reconnaissances of forward areas, and to meet units on arrival.

   1 Officer per Battalion.
   1 N.C.O. per Company.
   1 Private per Platoon.

6.. 6 lorries for the conveyance of baggage will rendezvous at LES CINQ CHEMINS (W.7.c.8.8.) at 7.30 a.m. on the 7th inst. 2 lorries are allotted to each battalion who will arrange for a responsible guide to be at LES CINQ CHEMINS at 7.30 a.m. to guide lorries to locations required.

7.. Brigade Headquarters will close at W.14.b.6.2. at 10.30 a.m. and re-open at SCHOOLS CAMP at an hour to be notified later.

8.. Acknowledge.

W Carr
Captain.
BRIGADE MAJOR.
102nd INFANTRY BRIGADE.

6:7:1918.
102 B.H.Q.

Distribution overleaf.

Distribution -

102nd Inf. Bde. Order No. 219

G.O.C.

Copy No. 1  G.O.C.
        2  Brigade Major.
        3  Staff Captain
        4  Intell. Officer.
        5  Bde. Transport Off.
        6  Signal Officer.
        7  1/4th Bn. Cheshire Rgt.
        8  1/7th Bn. Cheshire Rgt.
        9  1/1st Bn. Hereford Rgt.

       10  34th Division.
       11  O.C. No. 3 Coy. Train.
       12  Bde. Supply Officer.

       13  101st Inf. Bde.
       14  103rd Inf. Bde.
       15  208th Field Coy. R.E.
       16  A.P.M. 34th Div.
       17  O.C. 102nd L.T.M.B.
       18  102nd Field Ambulance.
       19  103rd Field Ambulance.

       20  Area Commandant, ST JANS TER BIEZEN.

Copies Nos. 21 & 22 - War Diary and File.

MARCH TABLE - to accompany 102nd Inf. Bde. Order No.: 219

STARTING POINT .. ROAD JUNCTION, E.15.c.10.10. (Sheet 27)

ROUTE - HOUTKERQUE - E.21.b. - Cross Roads E.28.d.5.3. - Cross Roads E.29.b.5.2. - ST. JANS TER BIEZEN.

| Serial No. | UNIT | From | To | Time head of column passes Starting Point. | ROUTE | REMARKS |
|---|---|---|---|---|---|---|
| 1. | 102nd Inf. Bde. Headquarters - Details 102nd L.T.M.B. .... | W.14.b.5.2. | SCHOOLS CAMP. | 10.15 AM | W.20.central - LA KRUYSTRAETE - R1.Junot. - E.1.d.1.6. - E.7.b. | |
| 2. | 1/4th Bn. CHESHIRE REGT. | HOFLAND AREA | -do- | 10.20 AM | Road E.3.c. - E.9.a. & c. - E.15.c.1.1. | |
| 3. | 1/7th Bn. CHESHIRE REGT. | BAMBECQUE. | -do- | 10.35 AM | LA KRUYSTRAETE - Road Junction E.1.d.1.6. - E.7.b. | |
| 4. | 1/1st Bn. HEREFORD REGT. | LES CINQ CHEMINS. | -do- | 11. AM. | Cross Roads W.19.b.2.6. - LA KRUYSTRAETE - Road Junction E.1.d.1.6. - E.7.b. - HOUTKERQUE. | |
| 5. | No. 3 Coy. Train .... | ROUSBRUGGE STATION. | -do- | 11.15 AM | LA KRUYSTRAETE - Road Junction E.1.d.1.6. - E.7.b. - HOUTKERQUE. | |

SECRET.

APP. 2(A)

## 102nd INFANTRY BRIGADE EXERCISE No. 1

Ref. Maps.
Sheets 27 N.E.
& 28 N.W. – 1:20,000.

9 : 7 : 1918.

1. The enemy heavily attacked the front of the IInd Corps this morning. The situation in the Battle Zone is obscure.

2. The 102nd Infantry Brigade with one Machine Gun Company will occupy the Right Sector of the EAST POPERINGHE line as soon as possible after dark to-night in accordance with Provisional Defence Scheme for Division in Corps Reserve and instructions issued from this office.

3. Units will move to positions by the following routes :–

   1/4th Bn. Cheshire Regt – to ~~Right~~ Left Sub-Sector – 7¹⁵
   Main Road L.10.a. & b. – Road Junction L.11.a.9.2. – SOUTH POPERINGHE SWITCH ROAD (avoiding ZWYNLAND BREWERY) – thence by tracks reconnoitred.

   1/~~7~~4th Bn. Cheshire Regt – to ~~Left~~ Right Sub-sector –
   Road L.10.a. & c. – Cross Roads L.16.a.45.80 – Cross Roads L.11.c.40.85 – Road Junction L.17.b.4.2.

   1/1st Bn. Hereford Regt – to Reserve – Any route leaving Camp after front line Battalions.

   Machine Gun Company – Any route S. of POPERINGHE.

4. Movement will be by platoons at 50ˣ interval.
   Units will not pass E. of the main POPERINGHE—ABEELE Road before 10.0 p.m.
   Units will be in position by midnight July 9/10th.

5. Completion of moves of Battalions and Machine Gun Company will be notified by units to Brigade Headquarters, ZWYNLAND BREWERY by the code word "SPOT".

6. Dress – Fighting Order.

7. Advanced Brigade Headquarters will open at ZWYNLAND BREWERY, L.12.c.1.4. at 10.30 p.m. 9th inst.

8. Acknowledge.

                                        M Carr   Captain.
                                        BRIGADE MAJOR.
102 B.H.Q.                              102nd INFANTRY BRIGADE.

Distribution –

| | |
|---|---|
| G.O.C. | 1/4th Bn Cheshire Regt. |
| Brigade Major | 1/7th Bn Cheshire Regt |
| Staff Captain | 1/1st Bn Hereford Regt |
| Intelligence Off. | O.C. 34th Div. M.G. Battn. |
| Signal Officer. | 34th Div. "G" (for information) |
| Bde. Transport Off. | Commandant, Right Sector. |

To accompany 102nd Inf. Bde.
EXERCISE No. 1

## Instructions regarding 102nd Inf. Bde. EXERCISE No. 1

1.. Strict silence will be observed during the march to and from positions. There will be no smoking.

2.. On receipt of the Code word "LEAVE" Battalions will march back to Camp by the same routes as those used for the march forward.

If possible time will allow of troops being W. of a North and South line through POPERINGHE on the return journey before it is light enough for ground or aerial observation. If this is not possible movement will have to be made by small units at wide intervals.

3... Units will notify this office the exact time they leave their present locations and will report taking up of of their dispositions in the line as soon as completed to enable a report to be drawn up as to the exact time taken over the movement.

4.. No transport or Lewis Guns will be taken.

5.. The line will be manned as it would be in action — Machine Gunners and Lewis Gunners manning the positions that are assigned to them.

6... O.C. Units are at liberty to change from routes or move their troops from any positions that are shelled.

7.. Each Battalion will send 2 runners to Brigade Headquarters, ZWYNLAND BREWERY by 10.30 p.m. These runners will know the way from Brigade to Battalion Headquarters.

8.. Battalions will forward a copy of their orders to this office and other battalions in the Brigade.

*M Carr*
Captain.
BRIGADE MAJOR.
102nd INFANTRY BRIGADE.

102 B.H.Q.
9:7:1918.

Distribution -

As for 102nd Inf. Bde. Exercise No. 1

SECRET.

T.S. 36/12

Reference Maps
Sheets 27 N.E. &
28 N.W. 1/20,000.

1.. With reference to para. 4 of Provisional Scheme for Division in IInd Corps Reserve forwarded to Battalions together with maps showing Corps and Divisional Boundaries, under this office letter T.S. 36/2 dated 3.7.18 - the Right Sector will be occupied as follows :-

(a) Right Sub-Sector -
From Southern Corps Boundary - G.15.c.1.6. - G.14.c.5.8. - G.13.central - L.17.b.5.2. - to inter-battalion boundary G.9.d.1.4. - G.8.d.5.7. - G.8.c.4.8. - thence along Light Railway (inclusive) to G.7.central.

1/4th Bn. Cheshire Regt -
  2 Companies ...... Front and Support Lines.
  Support Company ..... Reserve line.
  Reserve Company ..... G.8.c.

(b) Left Sub-sector -
From inter-Battalion boundary to the inter-Divisional boundary - G.10.a.7.9. - along YPRES--POPERINGHE Railway (exclusive) to G.3.c.8.1. - Cross Roads (exclusive) - G.3.c.2.9. - G.2.a.1.5. - A.25.d.2.2.

1/7th Bn. Cheshire Regt -
  2 Companies ...... Front and Support Lines.
  Support Company .... Reserve Line.
  Reserve Company .... G.8.b.

(c) 1/1st Bn. Hereford Regt. will be in Brigade Reserve and take up a position in L.11.d.

2.. Machine Guns -
9 Gun positions in the Right Sector, East POPERINGHE Line will be occupied by the Machine Gun Company attached from 34th M.G. Battn.

The positions to be occupied are as follows -

  G.14.b.8.2.    G.9.c.7.1.
  G.15.c.1.7.    G.9.c.9.2.  2 guns
  G.15.a.5.1.    G.9.c.8.7.
  G.15.a.4.4.    G.9.c.9.8.

4 guns will be held in Reserve near Brigade Hd. Qrs. in L.11.d. where O.C. M.G. Company will establish his H.Qrs. The position of the remaining 3 Guns will be notified later.

M Carr Captain.
BRIGADE MAJOR.
102nd INFANTRY BRIGADE.

6 : 7 : 1918.

Distribution of :-

T.S. 56/12

Copy No. 1  G.O.C.
         2  1/4th Bn. Cheshire Regt.
         3  1/7th Bn. Cheshire Regt.
         4  1/1st Bn. Hereford Regt.
         5  34th Div. M. G. Battn.
         6  101st Inf. Bde.
         7  103rd Inf. Bde.
         8  Sector Commandant, Right Sector.
         9  Staff Captain.

APP 1(B)

SECRET.                                                          Copy No ..

### 102nd INFANTRY BRIGADE ORDER No.. 220

                                                                11:7:1918.

1..   At 12 noon on July 11th the 30th American Division relieved
      the 34th Division of its responsibility for being ready to
man at short notice the EAST POPERINGHE System within the IInd
Corps boundaries.

2..   The 34th Division will remain responsible for roles (a) and
      (b) as laid down in para. (1) of Provisional Scheme for
Division in IInd Corps Reserve forwarded to Units of 102nd Infantry
Brigade under this office letter T.S. 36/2 dated 3.7.18.

3..   The Sector Commandant and guides Right Sector will remain
      in present locations and carry out duties laid down until
further orders.

                                                    Captain.
                                                BRIGADE MAJOR.
102 B.H.Q.                                    102nd INFANTRY BRIGADE.

Distribution -
        1/4th Bn. Cheshire Regt.      O.C. 102nd Bde. Signals.
        1/7th Bn. Cheshire Regt.      Staff Captain.
        1/1st Bn. Hereford Regt.      34th Division.
        102nd L. T. M. Battery.       Sector Commandant, Right Sector.

SECRET.  Copy No.. 17

APP 1c

## 102nd INFANTRY BRIGADE ORDER No.. 221

Reference Maps -
Sheet 27 N.E. : 1:20,000.    12 : 7 : 1918.
HAZEBROUCK 5A - 1:100,000.

1. The 102nd Infantry Brigade, less 102nd L.T.M.B., will move from SCHOOL CAMP to CORMETTE MUSKETRY CAMP on North side of the ST. MARTIN AU LAERT — ZUDAUSQUES Road 1½ miles South-West of TILQUES on the 13th instant.
   The dismounted portion will proceed by rail entraining at PROVEN STATION and detraining at ST. OMER, in accordance with Table "A" - and the mounted portion under O.C. No. 3 Coy. Train by road in accordance with Table "B" attached.

2. Each Battalion will detail one officer to report to the R.T.O. PROVEN STATION at 12 noon on the 13th instant to arrange accommodation in the train. He will take with him Entraining states for his Battalion.

3. Usual intervals will be observed on the line of march.

4. Lieut-Colonel Lawrence, D.S.O., Commanding 1/1st Battn. Herefordshire Regt. will be O.C. Train.

5. Advance parties from the 101st Infantry Brigade will report to Units on the evening of the 12th instant to take over SCHOOL CAMP. Targets and training stores will be handed over to those parties.

6. Staff Captain will issue instructions regarding Administrative arrangements.

7. The 102nd L.T.M.B. if not proceeding to the Corps School will remain at SCHOOL CAMP and be attached to and rationed by the 101st Infantry Brigade.

8. Brigade Headquarters will close at SCHOOL CAMP at 12 noon and re-open at CORMETTE at an hour to be notified later.

9. Acknowledge.

M Carr Captain.
BRIGADE MAJOR.
102nd INFANTRY BRIGADE.

Distribution -

| | | | |
|---|---|---|---|
| 1 | G.O.C. | 6 | 1/4th Cheshire Regt. |
| 2 | Brigade Major. | 7 | 1/7th Cheshire Regt. |
| 3 | Staff Captain. | 8 | 1/1st Hereford Regt. |
| 4 | Bde. Transport Officer .... | 9 | 102nd L.T.M.B. |
| 5 | O.C. 102 Bde. Signals .... | 10 | No. 3 Coy. Div. Train........ |
| 11 | Bde. Supply Off. | | |
| 12 | R.T.O. PROVEN. | | |
| 13 | 54th Division. | | |
| 14 | 101st Inf. Bde. | | |
| 15 | 103rd Inf. Bde. | | |
| 16 | Area Comdt., ST. MARTIN AU LAERT. | | |

17 & 18  War Diary & File.

TABLE "A" - To accompany 102nd Inf. Bde. Order No... 221

STARTING POINT .. Entrance to SCHOOL CAMP on main POPERINGHE—WATOU Road., L.3.a.8.4.

| Serial No. | UNIT | FROM | TO | Time head of each Unit passes Starting Point. | Route to PROVEN STATION. | TRAIN Time of departure. | TRAIN Time of arrival. | REMARKS. |
|---|---|---|---|---|---|---|---|---|
| 1. | 102nd Infantry Bde. H.Q. | SCHOOL CAMP. | CORNETTE | 11.15 a.m. 2.40 PM | L.3.b.9.5.— F.27.a.9.5.— Main PROVEN Road—PROVEN. | 2.0 p.m. 5.30 PM | 5.0 p.m. 7.30 PM | Units will march independently from Detraining Station. |
| 2. | 1/4th Bn. Cheshire Regt. | -do- | -do- | 11.20 a.m. 1.45 PM | [ST MARTIN AU LAERT SELLETTE] | -do- | -do- | -do- |
| 3. | 1/7th Bn. Cheshire Regt. | -do- | -do- | 11.30 a.m. 1.55 PM | | -do- | -do- | -do- |
| 4. | 1/1st Bn. Heref. Regt. | -do- | -do- | 11.40 a.m. 3.00 PM | | -do- | -do- | -do- |

375 Officers and Other Ranks of the 1/1st Bn. Herefordshire Regt. will proceed by the 6.45 a.m. personnel train from PROVEN (LENDINGHEM STATION) to-morrow, 13th instant. This party will report to the R.T.O. PROVEN STATION at 6.0 a.m. and will detrain at ST. OMER marching independently to CORNETTE.

TABLE "B" -- To accompany 102nd Inf. Bde. Order No... 221

STARTING POINT - ROAD JUNCTION, ST JANS TER BIEZEN - L.2.a.5.7.

| Serial No. | UNIT | FROM | TO | ROUTE | Time head of Units transport passes Starting Point. | REMARKS. |
|---|---|---|---|---|---|---|
| 1. | No. 5 Coy. Div. Train. | ST. JANS TER BIEZEN. | CORLETTE. | WATOU - WINIEZEELE - OUDEZEELE - ZEGLAERS-CAPPEL - L'HEY - CLAIRMARAIS - ST. OMER. | 7.0 a.m. | There is a suitable place for a midway halt North of the FORET DE CLAIRMARAIS midway between CLAIRMARAIS & HAUT SCHOUEBROUCK. |
| 2. | 102nd Inf. Bde. H.Q. | SCHOOL CAMP | -do- | -do- | 7.3 a.m. | -do- |
| 3. | 1/4th Bn. Cheshire Regt. | -do- | -do- | -do- | 7.6 a.m. | -do- |
| 4. | 1/7th Bn. Cheshire Regt. | -do- | -do- | -do- | 7.9 a.m. | -do- |
| 5. | 1/1st Bn. Hereford Regt. | -do- | -do- | -do- | 7.12 a.m. | -do- |

Administrative Instructions issued with 102nd Brigade Order No.221.
----------------------------------------------------------------

1. **EXTRA TRANSPORT.**

    7 lorries will report at 102nd Brigade Headquarters at 7-9am - 2 per Battalion - 1 per Brigade H.Q. Battalions will send representatives to take charge of their respective lorries. The lorries must leave SCHOOL CAMP before 9am and will go straight through to CORNETTE CAMP. Immediately they are unloaded they will report to the Staff Captain, 103rd Brigade to convey the baggage of the 103rd Infy Brigade to PROVEN.

    Baggage wagons and in addition the 2 Supply wagons per Battalion will report to Units at 4pm this afternoon. Baggage wagons will march with Units Transport. Supply wagons will be lightly loaded with any baggage not required and returned to No. 3 Coy Train today.

    The baggage loaded in the Supply Wagons will be unloaded at Supply Refilling Point near CORNETTE CAMP tomorrow and called for by 1st Line Transport the following day. Two men should accompany each Supply Wagon.

2. **SUPPLIES.**

    Supplies for consumption 14th instant will be delivered to units on the evening of the 13th instant. Supplies for consumption 14th and afterwards will be delivered to units by Supply Wagons.

    A proportion of dixies and the fresh meat for consumption tomorrow should be taken to the new area in the Motor Lorries so that a meal can be ready on arrival of the troops in Camp.

3. **LEAVE.**

    All personnel proceeding on leave on and after the 15th inst., will report to R.T.O. ST OMER at 5-30pm the day before they are due to Embark. Further instructions will be issued regarding this.

    O.R. proceeding on leave must be inspected by an Officer before leaving their Camp. Clothes, Boots, Rifles and Equipment must be clean, buttons polished and hair cut.

4. **CLEANLINESS OF CAMP.**

    Units are again reminded of the importance of leaving their Huts and Tents and Horse Lines scrupulously clean.

                                               for. Captain.
                                               Staff Captain.
                                               102nd Infantry Brigade.

12/7/18.

SECRET.

## 102nd INFANTRY BRIGADE ORDER No ... 222.

Reference Sheets -
27 N.E. 1:20,000.
19 S.E. 1:20,000.
5A HAZEBROUCK 1:100,000.

14 : 7 : 1918.

1. The 34th Division is in G.H.Q. reserve and will be prepared to move at short notice. It is possible that the Units first for entrainment will be required to commence entraining 8 hours after receiving the order to move.

2. If the Division is ordered to move by rail, Strategical Trains will be used. In that case the whole of the Division will be conveyed by train.

3. Entrainment for a move by Strategical Trains will be performed under the orders of Group Commanders. Groups will be composed as follows :-

   "X" Brigade Group -
   Commander G.O.C. Infantry Brigade at CORMETTE.
   Entraining Station - ST. OMER.
   The Infantry Brigade at CORMETTE.
   1 Coy. Div. Train, S.A.A. Section, D.A.C.

   "Y" Brigade Group -
   Commander G.O.C. Infantry Brigade at SCHOOL CAMP.
   Entraining Station - PROVEN.
   The Infantry Brigade at SCHOOL CAMP.
   1 Company Div. Train, H.Q. and "A" and "C" Coys 34th Bn. M.G. Corps, 208th Field Coy. R.E., 104th Field Ambulance, Divisional H.Q., H.Q. and No. 1 Sec. Div. Signal Coy., 2/4th Somerset Light Infantry (less 1 Coy.).

   "Z" Brigade Group -
   Commander G.O.C. Infantry Brigade at PROVEN.
   Entraining Station - WAAYENBURG (19/X.13.c.)
   The Infantry Brigade in PROVEN Area.
   1 Coy Div Train, "B" and "D" Coys 34th Bn. M.G. Corps, 207th and 209th Field Coys R.E., H.Q. Div. Train.
   103rd Field Ambulance, 44th Mob. Vet. Section.
   231st Employment Coy., H.Q. R.E., 102nd Field Ambulance,
   1 Company Somerset Light Infantry.

4. "X" Brigade Group will march to the Entraining Station in accordance with Table "A" attached. Zero hour will be notified to Units by wire.

5. Copy of 34th Division Administrative Instructions No. 52 is forwarded to 3 Battalions and No. 3 Coy. Train herewith.

   Acknowledge.

M Carr
Captain.
BRIGADE MAJOR.
102nd INFANTRY BRIGADE.

102 B.H.Q.
Distribution -
Copy No. 1  G.O.C.
     2  Brigade Major.              9   No. 3 Coy. Train.
     3  Staff Captain.              10  Bde. Supply Officer.
     4  Bde. Transport Off.         11  102nd L.T.M.B.
     5  O.C. 102 Bde. Signals.      12  34th Division "G".
     6  1/4th Cheshire Regt.        13  34th Division "Q".
     7  1/7th Cheshire Regt.        14  R.T.O. ST. OMER.
     8  1/1st Hereford Regt.        15  101st Inf. Bde.
                                    16  103rd Inf. Bde.
                                    19  C.R.A. 34 Div
     17 & 18 .. War Diary and File.

- 2 -

| Serial No. | Train No. | Ser. No. Division Table 'A' | UNIT | FROM | TO | Time head of Unit passes Starting Point | ROUTE | REMARKS |
|---|---|---|---|---|---|---|---|---|
| 7. | 4th Train | 10. | T'port 1/1st Bn. Herefordshire Rgt. less 1 Cooker and Team. | CORIETTE: MUSKETRY CAMP. | ST.OMER: STATION: | O plus 9 hrs. | ST.MARTIN AU-LAERT - ST.OMER. | |
| 8. | | 10. | 1/1st Bn. Hereford Regt. less 1 Coy. | -do- | -do- | O plus 10½ hrs | -do- | |
| 9. | 5th Train | 13. | No.3 Coy.Train - 1 Cooker & Team 1/7th Ches. Regt. 1 Cooker & Team 1/1st H'ford Regt. | -do- | -do- | O plus 12 hrs | -do- | No. 3 Coy. Train will join Column at ST. MARTINS-AU-LAERT. |
| 10. | | 13. | 1 Coy. 1/7th Bn. Cheshire Regt. 1 Coy. 1/1st Bn. Hereford. Regt. | -do- | -do- | O plus 13½ hrs | -do- | 'X' Brigade Group loading parties proceed by this train. |
| 11. | 6th Train | 18. | H.Q. & 1½ Sub-Sect. S.A.A. Section D.A.C. | To move under orders of C. R. A. | | | | |
| 12. | 7th Train | 19. | 1½ Subsections, S.A.A. Sect. D.A.C. | To move under orders of C. R. A. | | | | |

Time of passing Starting Point is based on Departure of train every three hours.

Table "A" – To accompany 102nd Inf. Bde. Order No. 222

STARTING POINT – CROSS ROADS 400x East of last E in CORBETTE.

Table 'A'.

| Serial No. | Train | Division | Ser. No. | UNIT | FROM | TO | Time head of Unit passes Starting Point. | ROUTE | REMARKS. |
|---|---|---|---|---|---|---|---|---|---|
| 1. | 1st Train | | 1. | 102 Inf.Bde.Transport: 102 Bde.Sig.Section Transport. 1-Cooker & team 1/4th Cheshire Regt. | CORBETTE: MUSKETRY CAMP. | ST. OMER STATION. | 0 hour. | ST.MARTIN AU-LAERT- ST.OMER. | Advance parties travel on this train. |
| 2. | 1st Train | | 1. | H.Q. 102nd Inf. Bde. Brigade Signal Section 102nd L.T.M.B. 1 Coy. 1/4th Ches.Regt. | -do- | -do- | 0 plus 1½ hrs. | -do- | 102nd L.T.M.B. will move with 101st Inf. Bde. so long as attached there. |
| 3. | 2nd Train | | 4. | T'port 1/4th Cheshire Regt. less 1 Cooker and Team. | -do- | -do- | 0 plus 3 hrs. | -do- | |
| 4. | 2nd Train | | 4. | 1/4th Cheshire Regt. less 1 Company. | -do- | -do- | 0 plus 4½ hrs. | -do- | |
| 5. | 3rd Train | | 7. | T'port 1/7th Cheshire Regt., less 1 Cooker and Team. | -do- | -do- | 0 plus 6 hrs. | -do- | |
| 6. | 3rd Train | | 7. | 1/7th Bn. Cheshire Regt. less 1 Coy. | -do- | -do- | 0 plus 7½ hrs. | -do- | |

– continued –

SECRET.

## ADDENDUM No. 1
## to
## 102nd. INFANTRY BRIGADE ORDER No. 223

15 : 7 : 18.

1. Dismounted portion of 102nd Infantry Brigade will entrain at ST. OMER and detrain at ROUSBRUGGE Station.

2. Units will move to entraining station in accordance with Table "B" below.

3. 375 Officers and Other Ranks of the 1/7th Bn. Cheshire Regt. will remain at CORMETTE MUSKETRY CAMP to-night and will proceed to the BAMBECQUE Area by the 12.30 p.m. train from ST. OMER to-morrow, 16th instant. They will report to the R.T.O. ST. OMER one hour before departure of train.

4. An entraining Officer from each Battalion will report to the Staff Captain forthwith.

5. Acknowledge.

M Parr Captain.
BRIGADE MAJOR.
102 B.H.Q.                 102nd INFANTRY BRIGADE.

---

## TABLE "B"

Starting Point – Western exit from Camp on the CORMETTE — ST. MARTIN AU LAERT Road.

| Ser. No. | UNIT | From | To | Head passes S.P. | ROUTE | TRAIN Dep. | TRAIN Arr. |
|---|---|---|---|---|---|---|---|
| 1. | 102nd Inf. Bde. H.Q. | CORMETTE | OOST CAPPEL | 2.40 pm | ST MARTIN AU LAERT– ST OMER. | 5.30pm | 8.30 pm |
| 2. | 1/4th Bn. Cheshire Regt. | –do– | HONDLAND. | 2.45 pm | –do– | –do– | –do– |
| 3. | 1/7th Bn. Cheshire Regt. | –do– | BAMBECQUE. | 2.55 pm | –do– | –do– | –do– |
| 4. | 1/1st Bn. Hereford Regt. | –do– | LES 5 CHEMINS ROUSBRUGGE CAMP. | 3.0 pm | –do– | –do– | –do– |

Units will march independently from Detraining Station.

102nd Infantry Brigade Headquarters will close at 2.30 pm at CORMETTE CAMP and open at OOST CAPPEL at an hour to be notified later.

SECRET.                                                    Copy No. 16


## 102nd INFANTRY BRIGADE ORDER No. 323

Ref. maps -
Sheets 19 & 27
1:40,000.
HAZEBROUCK 5A -                                         15 : 7 : 1918.
1:100,000.

1.      The 102nd Infantry Brigade will rejoin the 34th Division
to-day - Transport by march route - Dismounted portion by
Train.

2.      The 102nd Infantry Brigade will be accommodated in the
BAMBECQUE Area.

3.      Transport will move under O.C. No. 3 Coy. Div. Train in
accordance with Table "A" attached. Usual intervals will be
maintained on the line of march.

        Instructions regarding move of dismounted portion and
train arrangements will be issued later.

4..     Instructions regarding supplies, baggage lorries and
Administrative arrangements will also follow later.

5..     Entraining states showing total number of all ranks and
bicycles to be entrained will be forwarded to this office on
receipt of this order.

6..     Acknowledge.

                                              M Carr
                                                    Captain.
                                              BRIGADE MAJOR.
102 B.H.Q.                                 102nd INFANTRY BRIGADE.


        Distribution -


                Copy No. 1   G.O.C.
                        2    Brigade Major.
                        3    Staff Captain.
                        4    Bde. Transport Officer.
                        5    Bde. Signalling Officer.
                        6    1/4th Cheshire Regt.
                        7    1/7th Cheshire Regt.
                        8    1/1st Hereford Regt.
                        9    No. 3 Coy. Train.
                        10   Bde. Supply Officer.
                        11   R.T.O. ST. OMER.
                        12   Area Comdt. ST MARTIN-AU-LAERT.
                        13   34th Division.

                14 & 15  War Diary and File.

TABLE "A" - To accompany 102nd Inf. Bde. Order No... 225

STARTING POINT - CROSS ROADS 400 EAST of last E in CORMETTE.

| Serial No. | UNIT | From | To | Time head of Units T'port passes S.P. | ROUTE | REMARKS |
|---|---|---|---|---|---|---|
| 1. | 102nd Infantry Brigade H.Q. | CORMETTE CAMP | OOST CAPPEL. | 12.30 p.m. | ST.OMER - CLAIRMARAIS - L'HEY - WINNEZEELE - OUDEZEELE - HERZEELE. | |
| 2. | 1/4th Bn. Cheshire Regt. | - do - | HOFLAND | 12.32 p.m. | - do - | |
| 3. | 1/7th Bn. Cheshire Regt. | - do - | BAMBECQUE. | 12.35 p.m. | - do - | |
| 4. | 1/1st Bn. Hereford Regt. | - do - | LES CINQ CHEMINS ROUSBRUGGE CAMP. | 12.32 p.m. | - do - | |
| 5. | No. 3 Coy. Div. Train. | ST.MARTIN-AU-LAERT. | ROUSBRUGGE CAMP. | | - do - | No. 3 Coy. Train will join the column as it passes ST.MARTIN AU-LAERT. |

15 : 7 : 1918.
*******************

SECRET.  Copy No.. 1

## 102nd INFANTRY BRIGADE ORDER No.. 223

Ref. maps -
Sheets 19 & 27
1:40,000.
HAZEBROUCK 5A -   15 : 7 : 1918.
1:100,000.

1.      The 102nd Infantry Brigade will rejoin the 34th Division to-day - Transport by march route - Dismounted portion by Train.

2.      The 102nd Infantry Brigade will be accommodated in the BAMBECQUE Area.

3.      Transport will move under O.C. No. 3 Coy. Div. Train in accordance with Table "A" attached. Usual intervals will be maintained on the line of march.

        Instructions regarding move of dismounted portion and train arrangements will be issued later.

4..     Instructions regarding supplies, baggage lorries and Administrative arrangements will also follow later.

5..     Entraining states showing total number of all ranks and bicycles to be entrained will be forwarded to this office on receipt of this order.

6..     Acknowledge.

                                                M Carr
                                                    Captain.
                                            BRIGADE MAJOR.
102 B.H.Q.                              102nd INFANTRY BRIGADE.

Distribution -

         Copy No. 1   G.O.C.
                  2   Brigade Major.
                  3   Staff Captain.
                  4   Bde. Transport Officer.
                  5   Bde. Signalling Officer.
                  6   1/4th Cheshire Regt.
                  7   1/7th Cheshire Regt.
                  8   1/1st Hereford Regt.
                  9   No. 3 Coy. Train.
                 10   Bde. Supply Officer.
                 11   R.T.O.  ST. OMER.
                 12   Area Comdt. ST MARTIN-AU-LAERT.
                 13   34th Division.

              14 & 15 War Diary and File.

TABLE "A" - To accompany 102nd Inf. Bde. Order No... 225

STARTING POINT - CROSS ROADS 400 EAST of last E in CORMETTE.

| Serial No. | UNIT | From | To | Time head of Units T'port passes S.P. | ROUTE | REMARKS |
|---|---|---|---|---|---|---|
| 1. | 102nd Infantry Brigade H.Q. | CORMETTE CAMP | OOST CAPPEL. | 12.30 p.m. | ST.OMER - CLAIRMARAIS - I'KEY - WEIAERS CAPPEL - OUDEZEELE - HERZEELE - | |
| 2. | 1/4th Bn. Cheshire Regt. | - do - | HOFLAND | 12.32 p.m. | - do - | |
| 3. | 1/7th Bn. Cheshire Regt. | - do - | BAMBECQUE. | 12.55 p.m. | - do - | |
| 4. | 1/1st Bn. Hereford Regt. | - do - | LES CINQ CHEMINS. ROUSBRUGGE CAMP. | 12.38 p.m. | - do - | |
| 5. | No. 5 Coy. Div. Train. | ST.MARTIN-AU-LAERT. | ROUSBRUGGE CAMP. | | - do - | No. 5 Coy. Train will join the column as it passes ST.MARTIN AU-LAERT. |

15 : 7 : 1918.
****************

APPLE

SECRET.    Copy No. 24

**102nd INFANTRY BRIGADE**
**ORDER NO. 224**

Ref. Maps:
Sheet 27 1:40,000.
Sheet 19 1:40,000.

15 : 7 : 18.

1. 102nd Infantry Brigade Order No. 222 (issued to Units of original "X" Brigade Group) is cancelled.
   34th Division Administrative Instructions No. 52 attached to above order will hold good except for Table "A" and additions and amendments which will be notified by the Staff Captain.

2. The 34th Division will be transferred from the IInd Corps to the XXII Corps by rail.

3. "X" Brigade Group, which will move under the orders of G.O.C. 102nd Infantry Brigade will be composed as follows :-

   102nd Infantry Brigade.
   No. 3 Coy. Train.
   2/4th Bn. Somerset Light Infantry.
   H.Q. & 2 Sections 209th Field Co. R.E.
   "D" Coy. M. G. Battn.
   S.A.A. Section, D.A.C.

   Entraining Station ... REXPOEDE.

4. March to entraining station and entrainment will be carried out in accordance with Table "A" attached.
   The Staff Captain will superintend the entrainment at REXPOEDE Station and will travel by the train leaving at 4.50 p.m. on the 17th instant.

   Unit Commanders will ensure that Units arrive at the Station at the times given in the Table and that clear instructions are issued to detached parties proceeding on trains other than those on which the Unit Commanders are travelling.

5. 102nd Infantry Brigade Headquarters will close at OOST CAPPEL at 11.0 a.m. on the 16th inst. and re-open on arrival at destination.

6. 102nd L. T. M. B. will not move with the Brigade but will remain in present location.

7. Acknowledge.

M Carr  Captain.
BRIGADE MAJOR.
102nd INFANTRY BRIGADE.

102 B.H.Q.

Distribution -

| Copy No | | | | |
|---|---|---|---|---|
| 1 | G.O.C. | 11 | O.C. No. 3 Coy. Train. |
| 2 | Brigade Major. | 12 | Bde. Supply Officer. |
| 3 | Staff Captain. | 13 | 34th Division "G" |
| 4 | Bde. Transport Off. | 14 | 34th Division "Q" |
| 5 | Bde. Gas Officer. | 15 | R.T.O. RESPOEDE. |
| 6 | Bde. Signal Off. | 16 | 101st Inf. Bde. |
| 7 | O.C. 102nd L.T.M.B. | 17 | 103rd Inf. Bde. |
| 8 | 1/4th Cheshire Rgt. | 18 | C.R.A. 34th Div. |
| 9 | 1/7th Cheshire Rgt. | 19 | 2/4th Somerset L.I. |
| 10 | 1/1st Hereford Rgt. | 20 | 34th Bn. M.G.C. |
| | | 21 | 209th Field Co. R.E. |

22 & 23 ... War Diary & File.

SECRET

Copy No. 26

APPENDIX No 1 (c)

## 102nd INFANTRY BRIGADE ORDER No. 215.

15th June, 1918.

1.. The 34th Divisional Cadre (less all Battalion Cadres and Brigade Instructional Staff) will be transferred shortly to the First Army and will take over the training of the 80th American Division from the 16th British Division.

2.. (a) The 22nd Bn. Northumberland Fusiliers will hold itself in readiness to proceed to England at short notice with the 16th Division to be reconstituted.

(b) The affiliation of the 22nd Bn. Northumberland Fusiliers to the 308th Machine Gun Battalion will be taken over by the 23rd Bn. Northumberland Fusiliers who will attach their spare Company to the 308th Machine Gun Battalion on receipt of this order.

(c) The 22nd Bn. Northumberland Fusiliers will assist in the instruction of the 308th Machine Gun Battalion until such time as they depart.
The students at present attending the School under O.C. 22nd Bn. Northumberland Fusiliers will be transferred to the School of the 23rd Bn. Northumberland Fusiliers to-morrow, 16th instant. They will be accommodated by the 23rd Bn. Northumberland Fusiliers. The 22nd Bn. Northumberland Fusiliers will send instructors daily to the 23rd Bn. Northumberland Fusiliers School to assist in the instruction until date of departure.

3.. The remaining Battalion Cadres and Training Staffs of the 102nd Brigade will be transferred to the 39th Division at an early date and will remain in their present locations.

4.. The 102nd Infantry Brigade Headquarters and 22nd Bn. Northumberland Fusiliers Training Cadres will move with establishments authorised by 34th Division No. S/42 dated 7.5.1918 forwarded under this office letter A.37/3 dated 10.5.18.

5.. Acknowledge.

Captain.
for BRIGADE MAJOR.
102nd INFANTRY BRIGADE.

Issued at 12 noon -

### Distribution.

| Copy No. | | | |
|---|---|---|---|
| 1 | G.O.C. | 13 | 307th M.G. Bn. |
| 2 | Bde. Major. | 14 | 308th " |
| 3 | Staff Captain. | 15 | 309th " |
| 4 | Musketry Officer. | 16 | 309th M.G. Coy. |
| 5 | Bombing Officer. | 17 | 310th " |
| 6 | Signal Officer. | 18 | 311th " |
| 7 | Bde. Transport Off. | 19 | 312th " |
| 8 | Bde. Gas Officer. | 20 | 101st Inf. Bde. |
| 9 | 22nd N.F. | 21 | 103rd " |
| 10 | 23rd " | 22 | 34th Division. |
| 11 | 25th " | 23 | No. 3 Coy. Train. |
| 12 | 16th " | 24 | Bde. Supply Officer. |
| | | 25 | 34th Div. M.G. School. |

War Diary and File ... Copies 26 & 27.

B.M.

## 102nd Brigade Administrative Instructions No. 2.

Reference 102nd Brigade Order No. 224.

1. **ENTRAINING STRENGTHS.**

    All units will forward complete amended Entraining Strengths to Brigade Headquarters by 9am tomorrow, 18th July. Strengths will be shewn according to Trains and not according to complete units. Units proceeding by two trains will forward 2 separate states. The following particulars are required:-
    1. Officers.
    2. Other Ranks.
    3. Animals.
    4. 2 Wheeled Vehicles.
    5. 4 Wheeled Vehicles.
    6. Total Axles.
    7. Bicycles.

    Similar states will be taken by each unit to the Entraining Station.

2. With the exception of para. 8, 34th Divisional Administrative Instructions No. 52 hold good. A copy of 34th Division Administrative Instructions No. 53 is forwarded to 3 Battalions herewith for information.

3. **SUPPLIES.**
    Refilling for the following units will take place at 6am July 16 at the same Refilling Point near BAMBECQUE as existed when the Brigade was in the present area a fortnight ago.
    102nd Brigade H.Q.
    1/4th Bn. Cheshire Regt.
    1/7th Bn. Cheshire Regt.
    1/1st Bn. Hereford Regt.

    Supply wagons will return to units immediately after Refilling and will remain with them throughout the move.
    The Supplies refilled tomorrow are for consumption 20th inst.
    Supplies for consumption 17th, 18th & 19th will be dry rations. They will be dumped at REXPOEDE Station and will be picked up by units as they entrain.
    Units will arrange for their Quartermasters and Quartermaster Sergeants to accompany the Transport to Entraining Station to take over these Supplies and to distribute them amongst Companies.
    The usual A.B.55 will be submitted.

4. **BAGGAGE.**
    Unless orders are issued to the contrary all blankets will be taken to the Entraining Station and dumped at a place which will be shewn units on arrival.
    Only two lorries are available for the Brigade. They will work as follows:-

    Train No. 1.
        1. Brigade H.Q.     ) Report at 8am.
        1. 1/4th Cheshire Regt.)

    Train No. 2.
        2. for 1/4th Cheshire Regt.- Report on completion of 1 journey for No. 2 Coy Train.

    Train No. 3.    2. for 1/7th Cheshire Regt.
    Train No. 4.    2 for 1/1st Hereford Regt.
    Train No. 5.    1 for 1/7th Cheshire Regt.
                      1 for 1/1st Hereford Regt.

    Every effort must be made to load and unload these lorries quickly. They must on no account be detained by units or it will not be possible to use them as detailed.

(2).

5. ADVANCE PARTIES.    July 16th

The undermentioned Advance Parties will proceed by Train No. 1. at 2-50pm:- They will report to Officer in Charge of entraining 1½ hours before departure of the train:-

| | |
|---|---|
| Infantry Battalion. } | 1. Offr. & (1 per Battn H.Q. |
| Pioneer Battalion. } | 6 N.C.Os. 1 per Coy, 1 Transport |
| Machine Gun Coy | 1 Offr. 2 O.R. |
| Train Coy. | 1 N.C.O. |
| S.A.A. Section, D.A.C. | 2 N.C.Os.) Also an Officer |
| Field Coy R.E. | 2 N.C.Os.) if desired. |

6. LOADING PARTY FOR REXPOEDE STN.

The loading party will be found by 1 Coy 2/4th Somerset Light Infantry. This Coy will report to R.T.O., REXPOEDE Stn at 10-50am tomorrow, July 16th when billets will be arranged for them and their duties explained.

They will travel by train leaving REXPOEDE Station 4-50pm on July 17th.

7. UNLOADING PARTY AT DETRAINING STATION.

The unloading party will be found by 1 COY, 1/4th Cheshire Regt who will travel on the 1st train. They will report to R.T.O. at Detraining Station immediately on arrival when billets will be arranged and instructions given regarding their duties.

An escort of 25 men must accompany each Battalion & Transport to the Station.

Water Carts are to be entrained full.

Camp Kettles will be placed in the trucks so that at stations where hot water is available no time may be lost in getting tea.

A. B. Lsalle
Captain.
Staff Captain.
102nd Infantry Brigade.

15/7/18.

SECRET

**ATT G**

## 102ND INFANTRY BRIGADE NO.225.

REF.MAPS.
 BEAUVAIS
 SOISSONS 1/100,000                                    19/7/18


1. The 102nd Infantry Brigade will move today to the VEZ VAUMOISE Area (6 miles East of Crepy) dismounted personnel by lorry- mounted personnel and Transport by march route

2. 102nd Infantry Brigade Group will be composed as under:-

    102nd Inf.Brigade Headquarters
    1/4th Bn, Cheshire Regt,
    1/7th Bn, Cheshire Regt.
    1/1st Hereford Regt.
    2/4th Somerset Light Inf.
    208th Field Coy. R.E.
    "D" Co. 34th M.G.Batt
    102nd Field Ambulance
    No,3 Coy.Train

3. The dismounted personnel of 102d Bde Group will embus on the 19th inst. as follows-
    (a) Bde.H.Q.
        Embussing Point on main BOREST-BARON ROAD between "FM" due East of BOREST and Cross Roads 400x North of F in FONTAINE
        TIME - 6 a.m.

    (b) 1/4th Cheshire Regt,
        Embussing Point - main BOREST-BARON Road between "FM" due East of BOREST and Cross Roads 400x North of F in FONTAINE
        Time - 6 a-m-

    (c) 1/1st Hereford Regiment.
        Embussing Point - Main BOREST-BARON ROAD tail of column at BOREST
        Time - 6 a.m.

    (d) 1/7th Cheshire Regt.
        Embussing Point -MORTE FONTAINE-FONTAINE ROAD-head of column at FONTAINE.
        Time 6 a.m.

    (e) 102nd Field Ambulance
        Embussing Point -CHAALIS    Time:-6 a.m.

    (f) "D" Coy. M.G.Battn.    Embussing Point LA VICTOERE
        Time -6a.m,

    (g) 2/4th Bn, Somerset Light Infantry -Embussing Point Main SENLIS-BOREST Road West of MUNT L'EVEQUE
        Time 6 a.m.

    (h) 208th Field Co.R.E.
        Embussing Point VEILLE METRIE
        Time - 7 a.m.

4. Mounted personnel and transport will proceed by march route as follows:-
    ROUTE - BOREST-BARON-NANTUEIL-LEVIGNEN
    STARTING POINT - BARON CHURCH

| UNIT | Time head of column passes STARTING POINT |
|---|---|
| 102nd Inf.Bde.H.Q. | 6-40 a.m. |
| 1/4th Cheshire Regt | 6-45 a.m. |
| 1/7th Cheshire Regt | 6-50 a.m. |
| 1/1st Hereford Regt | 6-55 a.m. |
| 102nd Field Ambulance | 7-0 a.m. |
| "D" Coy. M.G.Bn. | 7-5 a.m. |
| 2/4th Somerset.L.I. | 7-10 a.m. |
| 208th Field Coy.R.E. | 7-15 a.m. |
| No.3 Coy.Train | 7-20 a.m. |

5. Each lorry will hold 18 all ranks
   Numbers for which accomodation are required:-

| | | |
|---|---|---|
| Inf.Battn.- | 20 Off. | 600 O.R. |
| Pioneer Bn. | 20 Off. | 500 O.R. |
| Field Co.R.E. | 100 all ranks | |
| M.G.Coy. | 6 Off. | 48 O.R. |
| | 8 guns | 5000 rounds S.A.A. |
| Field Ambulance | 2 Off. | 80 O.R. |

6. Any personnel surplus to above establishment will rendez-vous at BOREST by 10 a.m. today and report to Lieut.Donnelly attached Bde.H.Q.
   Buses will be available at 10 a.m. for 500 all ranks who will embus in accordance to be issued by Lieut.Donnelly

7. Dress- Full marching order Lewis Guns and 28. Drums will be carried on the buses
   S.A.A. to be carried 200 rounds Rations for 20th inst.and 2 petrol tins of water perplatoon to be carried on buses

8. Surplus kit will be dumped in present area-

9. 102nd Inf.Bde.H.Q. will close at BOREST at 5-45 a,m, and open at a time and place to be notified later.

10. Acknowledge by bearer

    Issued at 5 a.m.

                                            (sd)  M.CARR  Capt.
                                                  Brigade Major
                                                  102nd Inf.Bde.H.Q.

Didtribution:-

   Bde.H.Q.
   1/4th Cheshire Regt.
   1/7th Cheshire Regt.
   1/1st Hereford Regiment
   208th Field Co.R.E.
   102nd Field Amb.
   "D" Co. M.G.Bn.
   2/4th Somerset L.I.
   No-3 Coy.Train

Secret.                                                Copy No. 1
Ref Map.
SOISSONS         102ᵈ Bde. Orders No. 225.
1/100,000 Brulicity
                                                        20/7/18
Para I   The 102ⁿᵈ Infantry Brigade will
proceed by March Route to PAISEUX
(the Circular EH3 of to-day's date
sent to 3 Bns, & No 3 Coy Train.

   2  A Starting Point Road Junction just
North of "Facly" and south of VEZ.
       Unit                    Time head of
                               Unit Column
                               passes Starting Point.
   102ᵈ Bde. HQ                 11.20 P.m.
   O/C 1st 5th Herefordshire Rgt. 11.23 P.m.
   "  1/4th  "  Cheshire Rgt.   11.40 P.m.
   "  1/7   "  Cheshire Regt.   12.7 am
                                (21/7/18)
   No. 3 Coy. Divnl Train       12.24 am

2.

3. Route: VEZ – LARGNY – Road Junction 400x South of E in VILLIERS – COTTERETS "HALTE" 900x North of VILLIERS COTTERETS Village PUISEUX.

Units will halt ten minutes to the clock hour after passing the Starting Point.

1/4th Bn Cheshire Regt will have their first ten minute halt during their passing of Starting Point.

4. The 208th Field Coy. R.E. will join on to the rear of the Brigade Column at Road Junction 400x South of E in VILLIERS COTTERETS at 1.49am 21/7/18.

5. Copy of 34th Division Admn. Instruction No. 54 attached.

3

6. The 102nd Bde. Group composed as follows :-
    102nd Bde. Headquarters
    3rd Battalion
    No. 3 Coy Train
    208th Field Coy R.E.

7. Brigade H.Q. will close at VEZ at 11.0 P.m 20/7/18 & reopen at PUISEUX at an hour to be notified later.

8. 3 Battn & No. 3 Coy Train to acknowledge by bearer.

20/7/18        M Carr Capt
               Brigade Major
               102 Infantry Bde.

Issued at 10.30 P.m.
3 Battalion
No. 3 Coy Train
208th Field Coy R.E.
Bde. S.O.

C O P Y

SECRET  
Copy No,

## 102ND INFANTRY BRIGADE ORDER NO.226

REF.MAP  
    SOISSONS  
    (British Map)  
    1/100,000

20.7.18

1. The 102nd Infantry Brigade will proceed by march route today to PUISEUX (this cancels E.H.3 of to-days date sent to 3 Battalions and No,3 Coy.Train).

2. **STARTING POINT**–

   Road junction just North of "FACTY 400x SOUTH OF VEZ

| UNIT | Time head of Units column passes Starting Point |
|---|---|
| 102nd Brigade Headquarters | 11-20 p.m, |
| 1/1st Hereford Regt. | 11-23 p.m. |
| 1/4th Cheshire Regt. | 11-40 p.m. |
| 1/7th Cheshire Regt. | 12-7 a.m. 21/7/18 |
| No.3 Coy.Train | 12-24 a.m. 21/7/18 |

3. ROUTE.  
   VEZ – LARGNY – Road junction 400x South of C in VILLERS COTTERETS – "Halte" 900x North of VILLIERS COTTERETS VILLAGE – PUISEUX

   Units will halt 10 minutes to the clock hour after passing the Starting point.

   1/4th Bn,Cheshire Regiment will have their first 10 minutes halt during their passing of Starting point.

4. The 208th Field Coy.R.E. will join on to the rear of the Brigade column at road junction 400x South of C in VILLIERS COTTERETS at 1-49 a.m. 21/7/18.

5. Copy of 34th Division Administration Instructions No,54 attached

6. 102nd Bde.Group composed as follows:-  
       102nd Bde,Headquarters  
       3 Battalions  
       No,3 Coy.Train  
       208th Field Coy.R.E.

7. Bde.Headquarters will close at VEZ at 11.0 p.m. 20/7/18 and re-open at Puiseux at an hour to be notified later.

8. 3 Battalions and No,3 Coy.Train to acknowledge by bearer.

                                      (sd) M.CARR Capt.  
                                        Brigade Major  
                                        102nd Inf,Brigade

20/7/18  
Issued 10.30 P.M.  
    No, 3 Coy.Train    208 Field Coy.  
    3 Battalions    Bde Transport Officer

SECRET.

## 102nd INFANTRY BRIGADE ORDER No. 228

Copy No..

Reference Map
SOISSONS Sheet
(Fr) 1:80,000.

21st July, 1918.

1. (a) The enemy is holding approximately the line of the SOISSONS - CHATEAU THIERRY road. SOISSONS is in the hands of the enemy. BUSANCY and CHATEAU THIERRY are in the hands of the Allies.

    (b) The 34th Division now forms part of the 30th French Corps which holds the line roughly speaking from just West of COUTREMAIN to just East of PARCY TIGNY.
    The Southern boundary of the Corps is just North of the former place and the Northern boundary is just North of the latter place.

    (c) The 19th French Division is the Right Division of the 30th Corps, the 58th French Division is the right Division of the 20th French Corps which is on the left of the 30th Corps.

2. The 34th Division will relieve the 58th French Division during the 22nd and night of 22nd/23rd July. Relief to be completed before dawn on the 23rd July.
    102nd Infantry Brigade will take over the Left Sector of the 34th Divisional front with North and South boundaries in accordance with map issued to Battalions. This Sector will relieve the 4th Regiment, 38th Division.

3. The 102nd Infantry Brigade will march to-morrow, 22nd inst., to the FERME GRILLE in accordance with attached March Table. On arrival at this point, Units will be met by guides who will conduct them to preliminary positions at Ravine de SAVIERES West of MOULIN de VILLERS THELON. Special attention is drawn to the note at foot of March Table attached.

4. The whole of the Brigade Transport will march under orders of Brigade Transport Officer.

5. Locations of Infantry Transport Lines will be pointed out on arrival at FERME GRILLE or preliminary positions.

6. It is proposed to hold line as follows :-

    2 Battalions in Front Line disposed in depth.
    2 Companies in Front Line.
    1 Company in Support.
    1 Company in Reserve.

    1/1st Bn. Herefordshire Regt will take over Left Subsector of Left Sector of Divisional Front.
    1/7th Bn. Cheshire Regt. will take over Right Subsector of Left Sector of Divisional front.
    1/4th Bn. Cheshire Regt. will be in Support to this Sector.

7. O's. C. Battalions with their Company Commanders and Intelligence Officers and O's. C. Machine Gun Companies will be at FERME GRILLE at 9.0 a.m. 22nd instant to meet guides for purpose of reconnoitring their portion of the line.
    Commanding Officers of Battalions and Machine Gun Companies will meet the Brigadier at a time and place to be notified later after completion of their reconnoitring the line - to discuss and decide upon the actual system the line will be taken over.

8.. Gides will be ...

(2)

8. Guides will be provided by Outcoming troops to take forward Incoming troops.
They will meet Incoming troops at French Brigade Headquarters at time to be decided later.
All Officers - Platoon and Section leaders - must acquaint themselves during day with Routes from resting place to French Brigade Headquarters which is situated on road running East from MONTRAMBOEUF FARM and about 250X East of Farm where guides will be picked up.

9. The 102nd Infantry Brigade Headquarters will be at a location to be notified later.

10. Locations of Field Ambulances, Advanced and Main Dressing Stations, and Train Coys. will be notified later.
Rear Divisional Headquarters have closed at LARGNY and are now established at VIVIERES where they will remain until further orders.

11. Staff Captain will issue instructions as to Dumps, etc. later.

12. Medical Officers will make necessary arrangements with Outgoing troops for Forward Dressing Stations, etc.
Transport Officers, Quarter-master's will make themselves acquainted with all available troops forward.

Acknowledge.

H.G. Burdass Lt
for Captain.
BRIGADE MAJOR
102nd INFANTRY BRIGADE.

Distribution -

1. G.O.C.
2. Brigade Major
3. Staff Captain.
4. Bde. Transport Officer.
5. Bde. Signal Officer.
6. 1/4th Cheshire Regt.
7. 1/7th Cheshire Regt.
8. 1/1st Hereford Regt.
9. No. 3 Coy. Train.
10. Bde. Supply Officer.
11. "D" Coy. M.G. Battn.
12. 104th Field Ambulance.
13. 54th Division "G".
14. 208th Field Co. R.E.

15 & 16  War Diary and File.

March Table - To accompany 102nd Inf. Bde. Order No. 225

| Serial No. | UNIT | STARTING POINT | Time to pass Starting Point Personnel Transport | | ROUTE | DESTINATION |
|---|---|---|---|---|---|---|
| 1. | 102nd Inf. Bde. Headquarters | Cross Road's Ch VIVIERS | 8.0 a.m. | 8.0 a.m. | ROND DE LA REINE - TOUR RESIMONT - CARREFOUR DU S.DT DU CERF - MAISON FORRESTIER | Guides will meet each Group at the FERME GRILLE to guide it to preliminary positions. |
| 2. | 1/1st Battalion Herefordshire Regt. | PUISEUX Road | 8.5 a.m. | 8.5 a.m. | | |
| 3. | 1/7th Battalion Cheshire Regiment | ¼ mile West of PUISEUX | 8.12 am | 8.12 am | | |
| 4. | 1/4th Battalion Cheshire Regiment | | 8.32 am | 8.22 am | | |
| 5. | (W Coys, H. Q. Battn. (B and ¼ Coy. C) | | 8.42 am | 8.43 am | | |

Note: Halts at 10 minutes to clock hour.

Watches synchronised at 6.0 a.m.

Infantry will march through the woods alongside the route later on leaving the road available for vehicles which will follow the traffic regulations. These are as follows :- March on the right side of the road. Clear the roads when halted. No double banking.

S E C R E T

## 102ND INFANTRY BRIGADE ORDER No.228

REF.MAPS.
  OULCHY-LE-CHATEAU 1/20,000                                           23/7/18
  SOISSONS 1/80,000

1(a) The Xth French Army will attack at 5 a.m. on the 23rd inst. The principal attack of the XXX Corps of which the 34th Division forms a part will be made through LE PLESSIER HULEU on the ORME DU GRAND ROZOY, Ultimate objective BOIS D'ARCY.

 (b) The Corps on the left of the 34th Division will turn the BOIS D'HARTENNES from the North. The ultimate objective is MAAST-ET-VIOLAINE.

2(a) The role of the 34th Division is to attack on the front between BOIS DE CURJENNE - HARTENNES-ET-TAUX (both inclusive).

 (b) The ultimate objective is the BOIS D'ENCENS plateau of NEUVILLE ST.JEAN thus forming a connecting link between the division on the right of the 34th Division and the Corps on the left.

3. The attack of the 34th Division will not take place unless the attack of the Corps on its left is successful The infantry of the 102nd Brigade and Artillery will co-operate from zero hour by fire with due respect to expenditure of Ammunition.

4. The attack of the 34th Division when ordered will be carried out by the 101st Brigade on the right and the 102nd on the left.

5. The Artillery plan and orders for the signal for attack will be in accordance with copies of 34th Divn.G.25 issued herewith. Battalion and Company Commanders will ensure strict compliance with the orders contained therein.

6. When ordered the attack of the 102nd Infantry Brigade will be carried out in accordance with plan of attack attached. Any necessary changes in dispositions will be carried out on receipt of this order.

7. Gas helmets will be carried at the Alert. As many tools as possible will be carried forward for the consolidation of captured ground.

8. 102nd Infantry Brigade H.Q. will move forward to 855.457 (H.Q. 1/1st Bn.Hereford Regt.) on receipt of news of capture of first objective.

9. Acknowledge by bearer.                  (sd.) M.CARR Captain.
                                                                    Brigade Major
                                                                102nd Inf.Brigade.

Issued at 4 a.M.

| | | |
|---|---|---|
| G.O.C. | 1/4th Bn,Ches.Regt. | 103 F.A. |
| Staff Capt. | 1/7th Ches.Regt. | 101 Inf.Bde. |
| Sig.Off. | 1/1st Herefords. | 34 Divn. |
| Bde.T.O. | O.C."D" Co.,M.G.Batt. | 58th Fr.Divn. |

PLAN OF ATTACK

1. **101st Inf.Bde.**

   The initial moves in attack will be that the 101st Bde will attack and capture the BOIS DE CHANOIS and the woods to the North of it and establish itself in the sunken road which runs N. and S. immediately E. of these woods.

2. **102nd Inf.Bde.**
   (i.) The leading battalion 102nd Brigade (1/1st Bn.Hereford Regiment) will at the same time advance with its left in close touch with the right of the 58th French Division and capture the BOIS DE REUGNY by encircling it from the N. and S.

   (ii) During the movement the second battalion 1/7th Batt.Cheshire Regiment will move up to the southern flank of the 1/1st Bn, The Hereford Regiment and the two battalions will then move forward with the right and left flanks on dividing line as shewn on attached Map (forwarded to Battalions) and capture the first objective shewn on map in black and marked 1st,,,1st. When the capture of the first objective is complete the two leading Battalions will mop up the village and organise it against counyer-attack and gain touch with the 101st Brigade on their right (1/7th Bn,Cheshire Regt. responsible for this) and also touch with the 58th Division on their left (1/1st Bn,Hereford Regiment responsible)

   (iii) The third Battalion 1/4th Bn, The Cheshire Regiment will advance and pass through the 1/1st Bn,Hereford Regiment and 1/7th Bn,Cheshire Regt. who will be on the first objective and attack and capture the second objective which is shewn is black and marked 2nd...2nd. When capture is complete the 1/4th Bn,Cheshire Regiment will consolidate line shewn on attached map.

3. 
   (i) The 3rd Battalion of the 101st Bde wil advance when its leading Battalion has captured the BOIS DE CHANOIS and the 102nd Brigade has made good the Road junction 166 E. of BOIS DE REUGNY.

   (ii) During its advance its role will be to form a connecting link between the 101st and 102nd Brigades and eventually establish itself in Road ditch of the SOISSONS ROAD whence it will be able to cover the position taken up by the 101st and 102nd Brigades.

4. Orders will be issued for the advance to the ultimate objective BOIS DENCENS -Plateau of NEUVILLE ST.JEAN as occasion demands.

5. 
   (i) As soon as the 1/1st Bn,Hereford Regt and the 1/7th Bn, Cheshire Regiment move forward to the attack the 1/4th Cheshire Regt. will move forward and take up position in the trenches vacated by them ready to move forward

5. (ii) All Battalions will attack in depth O.'s.C. Battalions holding a small reserve of infantry and Machine guns.

6. The O.C. Machine Gun Company will get into touch with O.sC. Battalions to determine on role of guns.
More than four guns will be used in the initial stages of the
per battalion
attack Battalion Commanders holding at least four in reserve.

7. As soon as attack commences one Battalion of the Divisional reserve (consisting of one Battalion 103 Brigade 2/4th Somerset Light Infantry and half company machine guns) under command of Lt.Col.E.B.POWELL D.S.O.) will be moved foreard to covered ground west of PARCY TIGNY.

8. Units will forward copies of their orders as soon as possible to Brigade H.Q.

TABLE "A" -- To accompany 102nd. Infantry Brigade Order No. 224.

| Ser. No. | Date | UNIT | From | To | ROUTE | Time of arrival of unit at Entraining Station. | Time of dep. of train. | Remarks. |
|---|---|---|---|---|---|---|---|---|
| 1. | 16/7/18 | 102nd. Inf.Bde.T'port 102nd Bde.Sig.Sec." 1 Cooker & Team 1/4th Cheshire Regt. | OOST CAPPEL. | REMPOEDE STATION. | LES 5 CHEMINS - Main OOST CAPPEL-REMPOEDE Road. | 11.50 a.m. | 2.50 p.m. | |
| 2. | -do- | H.Q. 102nd. Inf.Bde. Bde. Sig. Section 1 Co. 1/4th Ches.Regt (unloading party) | OOST CAPPEL. HOMLAND | -do- | -do- | 1.30 p.m. | 2.50 p.m. | Advance parties of all units of "Y Bde. Group travel by this train. |
| 3. | -do- | T'port 1/4th Bn.Ches. Regt. less 1 Cooker and Team. | HOMLAND | -do- | LA KRUYSTRAETE - LES 5 CHEMINS | 2.50 p.m. | 5.50 p.m. | |
| 4. | -do- | 1/4th Bn. Cheshire Regt. less 1 Coy. | -do- | -do- | -do- | 4.20 p.m. | 5.50 p.m. | |
| 5. | -do- | T'port 1/7th Bn.Ches. Regt. less 1 Cooker and Team. | BANDEGNE | -do- | Road V.22.central - V.16.central - V.10.central. | 5.50 p.m. | 8.50 p.m. | |
| 6. | -do- | 1/7th Bn. Cheshire Regt. less 1 Coy. | -do- | -do- | -do- | 7.20 p.m. | 8.50 p.m. | |
| 7. | -do- | T'port 1/1st Hereford Regt. less 1 Cooker and Team. | ROUSBRUGGE CAMP. | -do- | Cross Roads V.19.b.2.6. - LES 5 CHEMINS. | 8.50 p.m. | 11.50 p.m | |
| 8. | -do- | 1/1st Bn. Hereford Regt. less 1 Coy. | -do- | -do- | -do- | 10.20 p.m. | 11.50 p.m | |

| Ser. No. | Date | UNIT | From | To | ROUTE | Time of arrl. of Unit at Entraining Station. | Time of dep. of Train | Remarks |
|---|---|---|---|---|---|---|---|---|
| 9. | 17/7/18 | No. 3 Coy. Div. Train ............ | ROUSBRUGGE CAMP. | REXPOEDE STATION. | Cross Roads J.19.b.2.6. LES CINQ CHEMINS | 12.50 a.m. | 3.50 a.m. | |
| | | 1 Cooker and team 1/7th Bn. Cheshire Regt. 1 Cooker and team 1/1st Bn. Hereford. Regt. | BAMBECQUE. ROUSBRUGE CAMP. | | As for Ser. No.5 As for Ser. No.7 | | | |
| 10. | -do- | 1 Co: 1/7th Ches. Regt. 1 Co: 1/1st Hereford. Regt | BAMBECQUE. ROUSBRUGE CAMP | -do- | -do- | 2.20 a.m. | 3.50 a.m. | |
| 11 | -do- | H.Q. & 1½ Sub-Sections S.A.A. Sec. D.A.C. ... | Under orders to be issued by G.R.A. | | | | 3.50 a.m. | |
| 12. | -do- | 1½ Sub-sections S.A.A. Sec. D.A.C. ......... | | -do- | | | 10.50 a.m. | |
| 13 | -do- | T'port 2/4th Somerset L.I. less 1 Cooker and team ...... | Present Location. | -do- | Any | 10.50 a.m. | 1.50 p.m. | |
| 14. | -do- | T'port 2 Sections 209th Field Co. R.E. ..... | -do- | -do- | -do- | 12.20 p.m. | 1.50 p.m. | |
| 15. | -do- | 1 Cooker and team 2/4th Bn.Somerset L.I. T'port "D" Coy. ½ G.Bn. | Present location | -do- | -do- | 1.50 p.m. | 4.50 p.m. | |
| 16. | -do- | H.Q. & 2 Sections 209th Field Co. R.E. 1 Coy. 2/4th Somerset L.I. (loading party) "D" Coy. M.G. Battn. | -do- | -do- | -do- | 3.20 p.m. | 4.50 p.m. | |

SECRET                                                              No.5

## 102 INFANTRY BRIGADE ORDER NO.229

REF. MAPS
   OULCHY-LE-CHATEAU 1/20.000
   SOISSONS 1/80,000                                      27-7-18

1. The 34th Division will be relived by French troops on the night July 27/28th.

2. The 350th Infantry Regiment of the 12th Division will take over the line from point 99.30 to the northern boundary of the 34th Division relieving the 102nd Infantry Brigade and troops of the 101st Brigade in the line from the 102nd Brigade Southern boundary to point 99.30.

3. Battalions will be relived as under:-

1/7th Bn, Cheshire Regiment Right front battalion by two Companies of the Battalion de NOUAILLAN S.
Troops of the 101st Brigade between 102nd Brigade/boundary and point 99.30 by one Company of the battalion de NOUAILLAN
1/4th Bn, Cheshire Regiment Left front Battalion by three Companies of the Battalion de COSTEUR
1/1st Hereford Rgt. Reserve battalion by three companies of the Battalion de TARLE.

   Each French Battalion will have eight Machine Guns attached.

4. Guides for relieving troops will be found as follows :-

(a) 2 guides per French company from 1/7th Bn, Cheshire Regiment and battalion form 101st Infantry Brigade to be at cross roads 71.42 at 10.30 P.M. to meet the Battalion de NOUAILLON Route along valley to PARCY TIGNY.

(b) 2 guides per French Company from 1/4th Bn, Cheshire Regiment to be at the junction of five roads 72.51 at 10.30 p.m. to meet the Battalion de COSTEUR-Route main VIERZY-TIGNY road.

(c) 2 guides per French company from 1/1st Bn, Hereford Regiment to be at cross roads 88.49 at 10.30 p.m, to meet the Battalion de TARLE which is being relieved in the French front line tonight. Platoon and post guides will meet companies at a place to be arranged between O.sC British and French Battalions.

4.(d) MACHINE GUNS:-

    1 guide for four guns for right front battalion 102nd Bde
    1 guide for four guns for battalion of 101st Bde.
    2 guides for eight guns for left front Battalion
    2 guides for eight guns for Reserve Battalion.

    To be at the same rendez-vous as given for Battalions above O.C."B" Coy M.G.Battalion will arrange.

5. On relief the 102nd Bde. will proceed to the Eastern portion of the BOIS DE NADON Route Road passing Eastern edge of BOIS DE MAULOY-BLANZY-BOIS DE NADON

6. The two mounted officers sent from each Battalion in accordance with instructions issued will be responsible for guiding battalions to new area. Additional guides will be sent forthwith to reconnoitre the route laid down.

7. All British ammunition and stores will be removed from the area. All stores taken over from the French will be handed back on relief.

8. Completion of relief will be reported to this office by wire by code word "FATTY".

9. 102nd Brigade H.Q. will close at present location and re-open at a place and time to be notified later.

10. The command of the Brigade Sector will pass to the Officer Commanding the 350th French Infantry Regiment at 2 a.m. on July 28th

11. ACKNOWLEDGE.

                        (sd) M.Carr    Capt.
                        Brigade Major
                        102nd Inf,Brigade.

Issued at 4.30 p.m.

1. G.O.C.
2. B.M.
3. Staff Captain
4. Bde.Sig.Officer
5. 1/4th Cheshire Regiment
6. 1/7th Cheshire Regiment
7. 1/1st Hereford Regt,
8. O.C."B" Coy.M.G.B.
9. 34th Division
10. 101 Bde.
11. 103 Bde
12. O.C. 350th French Inf.Regt.
13. 103 Field Ambulance.

SECRET　　　　　　　　　　　　　　　COPY No

## 102ND INFANTRY BRIGADE ORDER No 230

Refce Maps
　OULCHY-LE CHATEAU 1/20,000
　FERE-EN-TARDENOIS 1/20,000　　　31.7.18

1(a) The 34th Division will resume the attack to-morrow morning August 1st

(b) The objectives, Divisional & Brigade boundaries are shown on the attached Map (issued to Battns only)

(c) The attack will commence at ZERO hour to be notified later

(d) The 30th & 11th French Corps are attacking at the same time
30 Tanks are co-operating & will probably cross the Divisional Front from the Left

2. The 103rd Infantry Brigade will attack on the right of the Divisional Front

GS.286/113　　9.50 p.m. 31.7.18

2

and the 101st Inf. Brigade on the Left.
The 102nd Infantry Brigade will be in Divisional Reserve.

3. ASSEMBLY
(a) The 101st & 103rd Infantry Brigades will take up fighting formations with their leading waves as close as possible to the starting line shown on map attached. The two attacking brigades will extend their inner flanks to the Inter-Brigade Boundary & will then move to battle positions.

(b) 1/7th Battn. Cheshire Regt (less 1 coy & 1 platoon) will assemble in the PARIS line just N. of the BOIS DU MONCEAU. The company holding the line of advanced posts will not be withdrawn. One platoon will also remain in close support to the outpost company. The attacking troops will pass through the line of posts.
This company & platoon will rejoin

3.

their Battalion when the latter moves forward & passes through them.

(c) 1/4th Battn Cheshire Regt will remain in present location just S of BOIS DU MONTCEAU

(d) 1/1st Battn Herefordshire R will withdraw to the PARIS Line immediately South of that portion occupied by the 1/4th Battn Cheshire Regt

(e) 2/7th Bn. Som Light Inf will move from the BOIS DE LA BAILLETTE to the portion of the VERS - SOISSONS Ry between the Inter-Brigade & Southern Divisional Boundary as soon as possible after dark

(f) The withdrawal of the 1/1st Bn Herefordshire Regt & the 1/4th Battn Cheshire Regt (with the exception of 1 Coy & 1 Platoon) from East of the PARIS LINE will not take place until OsC Coys are satisfied that troops of attacking Brigades are in their Assembly Positions

4

(g) Battalions will report completion of Assembly by Code Word "BULLET". (by wire if possible)
Assembly must be completed by midnight 31st/1st.

4 ACTION OF INFANTRY

(a) The Infantry of attacking Brigades will advance at ZERO hour
The 102nd Inf. Bde. will be standing-to ready to advance by ZERO hour

(b) The 1/4th Battn Cheshire Regt will advance immediately in rear of the last waves of the 101st Brigade & will attack and capture LA MONT TOUR
This Battalion will detail two platoons each complete with L.L.G. — one platoon to occupy Copse immediately South of LA MONT TOUR — the other to occupy Copse W. of Point 199

The 1/1st Battn Herefords Regt will advance immediately in rear of the 103rd Brigade's last waves

5

and attack & capture BUCY LE
BRAS FERME
This Battalion will detail one
platoon complete with 2 L.G. to
occupy the two copses N.E. of Point
172

These moves are to secure the flanks
of a French Division passing through
the 34th Division in a Northerly
direction.
The platoons detailed for occupying
copses will only be required in
the event of attacking Brigades
failing to occupy them

The 1/4th Battn Cheshire R will
get into touch with troops of the
25th French Division & the 1/1st
Battn Herefordshire Regt with troops
of the 68th French Division.
These Divisions are operating on the
left & right of the 34th Division
respectively.

5 ACTION OF ARTILLERY & MACHINE GUNS
(a) The artillery barrage will advance
at the rate of 100 yards in 3 mins

without a pause until it has passed the objective (BROWN LINE). It will remain beyond that line for 30 mins when it will cease. The role of Artillery will then be to cover the consolidation of the position & support further advance.

(6) Machine Guns will give covering fire from the BOIS DU MONTCEAU.

6 Red flares (which are being issued to-night) will be used in addition to flarets to give the position of foremost troops to aeroplanes to-morrow.

7 Brigade H.Q. will remain in present location & will move forward during the advance to the PARIS LINE about 300x S of the BOIS DU MONTCEAU at a time to be notified later.

7.

8. The 1/7th Battn Cheshire R & 2/4th
Battn South L. will not move
from Assembly Positions without
orders from B.G.C. 102nd Inf
Bde.

9. ACKNOWLEDGE by wire/phone

M Carr Capt
for Major
¼ 2nd Inf Bde.

Zero hour will be at 4.45 A.M.
August 1st

Copies of Verbal orders given
to special reasons are attached

84 Div G. for information

5/4          Copy                July 31.
                                    9 p.m.

1/4 C  2/4 Somersets

You will please detail tonight
1 Officer and 1 Section men and
attach 3 good Signallers to this
party.

The Officer must be able to talk French.

He will report to C.O. of the Right
Battalion of the 18th Division.
It will be a battalion of the 355th
Regiment of Infantry (French)

He and party will remain with this
Battn till after operation.

The Division will be forming up in
rear of Ribly.
            This Officer and party
must report to the French Battn by
4.15 a.m.

Please send this officer to
see me now.
                    Sgd/ Edward William
                              B.G.C.
9.50 pm

E.H.Q.    Copy    July 31st
                              7 p.m.

To:  O.C. 1/4 Cheshires

i/   You will detail a special party
under an officer (1 Sec. O.R. and 3 good
Signallers) to keep in touch with a
Special Liaison Group sent to a French
Division (124) – The Liaison Group
attached to French Div. belongs to
the 2/4th Somersets.

ii/  Your party will accompany your
Bn. to your objective which is
LE MNT JOUR – On arrival
there he will get in touch by Signals
with the French Div. who will be
eventually passing through us.
He will remain in touch during the
operation.
        He is practically a
Liaison Post.

iii/ The French Div. 124 will be in
position West of Rly. by 4.30 a.m.

Acknowledge.
                    Sgd/ Edward Bell
                           B.G.C. 1/2

Secret.                    **102nd INFANTRY BRIGADE ORDER No.** 230     Copy No.

Ref. Maps -
OULCHY LE CHATEAU - 1:20,000
SOISSONS, S.E., 1:50,000.
SOISSONS, 1:80,000.

APP 12

28th July, 1918.

1. The 34th Division will carry out an attack on the enemy at zero hour (to be notified later) on the 29th inst. in conjunction with French troops on its right and left.

2. A copy of 34th Division Instructions No. 1 giving dispositions of Division for the attack is forwarded to Battalions of the 102nd Infantry Brigade.

3. The 102nd Infantry Brigade less 1 Battalion will be in Divisional Reserve.
   The 1/4th Bn. of the Cheshire Regt. will be in Corps Reserve.

4. Units of the 102nd Infantry Brigade will move to positions of assembly in accordance with Table "A" attached.

5. Distances to be observed on the line of march will be as follows -

   50x between platoons.
   100x between Companies and Battalions.

   Company limbers, Field Kitchens and Pack Mules will march in rear of their Companies. Other transport in rear of Battalion.

   Strictest discipline will be observed.

   Box respirators will be carried at the alert.

6. Limbers will be unloaded in the ravine just W. of the BOIS DE LA BAILLETTE.
   The following will remain with units :-

   Water carts.           Field Kitchens.
   Pack animals.          Lewis Gun Limbers.
   Officers chargers.

   Battalion tools will be taken to position of assembly - either on the man or by limber for issue there.
   O's. C. Battalions and Adjutants only will be mounted.

7. One French guide will meet each Battalion at FME. DE FRONTENY and guide it to assembly position.

8. All ranks will be warned to give immediate response to calls from aeroplanes to show position. The signal is a light bursting into 6 white lights. Troops in the front line only will respond to the signal.

9. Administrative instructions will be issued by the Staff Captain.

10. Brigade Headquarters will close at FME DE BELLEVUE at 10.0 p.m. and open just North of the first B in BOIS DE LA BAILLETTE at an hour to be notified later.

11. Acknowledge.

                                            ........ Captain.
Issued at                                   BRIGADE MAJOR.
Distribution.                               102nd INFANTRY BRIGADE.
Copy No. 1  G.O.C.
        2  B.M.              8   O.C. 2/4th S.L.I.
        3  Staff Captain.    9   C.R.E. 34th Div.
        4  Intell. Off.      10  O.C. 34th M.G. Battn.
        5  Bde. Signal Off.  11  1/4th Ches. Regt.
        3  Bde. Supply Off.  12  1/7th Ches. Regt.
        7  Bde. Transport Off. 13 1/1st Hereford Regt.
                             14  34th Div.
        15 & 13  .. War Diary and File.

To accompany 102nd Inf. Bde. Order No... 230.

Starting Point -X Road Junction - 5903 (Point 132) - (OULCHY LE CHATEAU)

| Serial No.: | Date | UNIT | From | To | Time head of Units: column passes Starting Point. | Route | Remarks. |
|---|---|---|---|---|---|---|---|
| 1. | 30:7:18 | 102nd Inf. Bde. H.Q. Qrs...... | BOIS DE MADON. | Just N. of 1st B in BOIS DE LA BAILLETTE. | 10.40 p.m. | ST. REMY BLANZI Fm. DE FRONTENY. | |
| 2. | -do- | 1/1st Battn. Hereford Regt... | -do- | Area just North of BOIS in BOIS DE LA BAILLETTE. | 10.42 p.m. | -do- | Will halt when passing Starting Point |
| 3. | -do- | 1/7th Battn. Cheshire Regt... | -do- | Area just South of BOIS IN BOIS DE LA BAILLETTE. | 11.7 p.m. | -do- | |
| 4. | -do- | 1/4th Battn. Cheshire Regt... | -do- | North-West corner of the BOIS DE LA BAILLETTE. | 11.22 pm | -do- | Corps Reserve. |

SECRET  COPY NO. 17

## 102ND INFANTRY BRIGADE ORDER NO. 231

31-7-18

REF. MAPS
OULCHY-LE-CHATEAU 1/20,000
FERE-EN-TARDENOIS 1/20,000

1. (a) The 34th Division will resume the attack tomorrow morning August 1st.

   (b) The objectives Divisional and Brigade boundaries are shewn on the attached map (issued to battalions only)

   (c) The attack will commence at ZERO hour to be notified later.

   (d) The 30th and 11th French Corps are attacking at the same time. 30 Tanks are co-operating and will probably cross the Divisional front from the left.

2. The 103rd Infantry Brigade will attack on the right of the Divisional front. and the 101st Infantry Brigade on the left. The 102nd Infantry Brigade will be in Divisional Reserve.

3. ASSEMBLY

   (a) The 101st and 103rd Infantry Brigades will take up fighting formations with their leading waves as close as possible to the starting line shewn on map attached. The two attacking Brigades will extend their inner flanks to the inter-Brigade Boundary and will then move to battle positions.

   (b) 1/7th Battalion Cheshire Regiment (less one company and one platoon) will assemble in the PARIS LINE just N. of the BOIS DU MONTCEAU. The company holding the line of advanced posts will not be withdrawn. One platoon will also remain in close support to the outpost Company. The attacking troops will pass through the line of posts.
   This company and platoon will rejoin their battalion when the latter moves forward and passes through them.

   (c) 1/4th Bn, Cheshire Regiment will remain in present location just S, if he BOIS DU MONTCEAU.

   (d) 1/1st Bn, Hereford Regt, will withdraw to the PARIS LINE immediately South of that portion occupied by the 1/4th Bn, Cheshire Regiment.

   (e) 2/4th Bn, Somerset Light Infantry will move from the BOIS DE LA BAILLETTE to the portion of the VERS-SOISSONS RLY between the inter Brigade and Southern Divisional Boundary as soon as possible after dark.

   (f) The withdrawal from East of the PARIS LINE of the 1/1st Hereford Regt. and the 1/7th Cheshire Regiment (with the exception of 1 Coy. and 1 Platoon) will not take place until Officer Commanding are satisfied that troops of attacking Brigades are in their Assembly positions.

   (g) Battalions will report completion of assembly by code word "BULLET" (by wire if possible),
   Assembly must be completed by mid-night 31/1/-

-2-

4. ACTION OF INFANTRY
   (a) The infantry of attacking Brigades will advance at zero hour, The 102nd Infantry Brigade will be standing to ready to advance by ZERO hour

   (b) The 1/4th Bn, Cheshire Regt, will advance immediately in rear of the last wave of the 101st Brigade and will attack and capture LA MONT JOUR.
   This Battalion will detail two platoons each complete with 2 L.G's - one platoon to occupy copse immediately South of LA MONT JOUR - the other occupy Copse W of Point 199

   The 1/1st Bn, Hereford Regiment will advance immediately in rear of the 103rd Brigades last waves and attack and capture BUCY LE BRAS FERME
   This Battalion will detail one platoon complete with 2 L.G's. to occupy the two copses N.E. of Point 172
   These moves are to secure the flanks of a French Division passing through the 34th Division in a Northerly direction.
   The platoons detailed for occupying the copses will only be required in the event of attacking Brigades failing to occupy them.
   The 1/4th Bn, Cheshire Regiment will get into touch with troops of the 25th French Division and the 1/1st Hereford Regt with troops of the 68th French Division.
   These Divisions are operating on the left and right of the 34th Division respectively.

5. ACTION OF ARTILLERY AND MACHINE GUNS
   (a) The artillery barrage will advance at the rate of 100 yds in three minutes without a pause until it has passed the objective (BROWN LINE)
   It will remain beyond that line for 30 mins. when it will cease. The role of the Artillery will then be to cover the consolidation fo the position and support further advance.

(6) Machine Guns will give covering fire from the BOIS DU MONTCEAU

   Red flares (which are being issued tonight) will be used in addition to panels to give the position of foremost troops to aeroplanes tomorrow.

7. Brigade Headquarters will remain in present location and will move forward during the advance to the PARIS LINE about 300 x S. of the BOIS DU MONTCEAU at a time to be notified later.

8. The 1/7th Bn, Cheshire Regiment and the 2/4th Bn, Somerset L.I. will not move from assembly positions without orders from B.G.C. 102nd Inf, Bde.

9. ACKNOWLEDGE by wire.

                                              (sd) M.CARR   Capt.
                                              Brigade Major
                                              102nd Inf, Brigade.

Zero hour will be at 4-45 A.M. August 1st.

28031 W3125/M2250 1000m 6/17 M.R.Co.,Ltd. (1367) Forms W3091.        Army Form W. 3091.

# Cover for Documents.

---

Nature of Enclosures.

---

Notes, or Letters written.

VOL. XXXIII.

# WAR DIARY
## 102ND INFANTRY BRIGADE H.Q.
## AUGUST - 1918

*Edward Hilliam*
BRIGADIER GENERAL
CDG. 102ND INFANTRY BRIGADE

10:9:18

Army Form C. 2118.

# WAR DIARY
## or
## INTELLIGENCE SUMMARY.
(Erase heading not required.)

SHEET 1   VOLUME

REF MAPS $\frac{1}{80,000}$ OULCHY LE CHATEAU

Instructions regarding War Diaries and Intelligence Summaries are contained in F.S. Regs., Part II. and the Staff Manual respectively. Title pages will be prepared in manuscript.

| Place | Date | Hour | Summary of Events and Information | Remarks and references to Appendices |
|---|---|---|---|---|
| PARIS LINE | Aug 1st | 3.30 AM | Left trenches approx 150" Soft BOURDON GRAND ROSOY ROAD | REF. OULCHY LE CHATEAU FERE-EN-TARDENOIS |
| | | 4AM | One battery on retreat to rearward | |
| | | 4.15 | The retreat commenced with 2 company returns to rearward to... line first two companies BEAUVIEUX BOURDON 23 O'clock | |
| | Aug 2nd | 6.30AM | Mont Le Tour remaining ... the offensive line guns with 6 HE enemy gunfire | |
| | | | Position 1/1 HERGFORD BRO PARIS LINE | |
| | Aug 3rd | 10AM | 1/2 4th Battle REF. BATTERY RGS. ... 450 x 25 T BEAUVOIR PARIS LINE | |
| | | | ... salvage work carried out the gun teams working to ... transport to rear | APP I (A) |
| SOUVRE-LA-LOUIS | Aug 4 | | Brigade returned at NANTEVIL ... | BEAUVOIS |
| | Aug 5 | | Bien at No 232 issued with respect to 72 hrs or rail | APP (6) |
| REMIGNY CAPPEL | Aug 8 | | ... at BEAUVOIS ... 8 TARDENOIS ... L DONTON CAPPEL | |

Army Form C. 2118.

# WAR DIARY
## or
## INTELLIGENCE SUMMARY.
(Erase heading not required.)

Instructions regarding War Diaries and Intelligence Summaries are contained in F. S. Regs., Part II. and the Staff Manual respectively. Title pages will be prepared in manuscript.

| Place | Date | Hour | Summary of Events and Information | Remarks and references to Appendices |
|---|---|---|---|---|
| EVERE CAPPEL | Aug 8 | | Interior economy carried out by Battalions. | HAZE BROUCK |
| | Aug 9 | | Inspection of the Bn by the G.O.C. 102nd Inf Bde. | |
| | Aug 10 | 4.45 pm | Warning order Received from Divn for the Bde to be ready to move to "la" HERZEELE area on 13th Aug 1918 | |
| | Aug 11 | | Training carried out by the Battalion | |
| | Aug 12 | | Training, Advance parties left for HERZEELE area to prepare to move to HERZEELE. Operation order No 235 issued. | APPX (B) |
| HERZEELE | Aug 13 | | Brigade moved by road route leaving ESCOELBECQ & WORMHOUDT & arriving HERZEELE 11.30 pm. Bn are Billeted as follows Bde HQ HERZEELE 1/4 HEREFORD REGT HARZEELE D A & 6.7 Coys 1/4 CHESHIRE REGT D Q & C Coys 1/4 CHESHIRE | 2 Officers Capt. T. J. HISLOP from Bn are attached to 1/4 HEREFORD REGT HARZEELE. |
| | Aug 14 | | Training carried out by the Bn. Arrangements made for the use of the Bois St PIERRE Rfle School for training purposes commenced. | |
| | Aug 15, 16, 17 | | Training carried out at Bois St PIERRE. | |

# WAR DIARY
## or
## INTELLIGENCE SUMMARY

Army Form C. 2118.

*(Erase heading not required.)*

Instructions regarding War Diaries and Intelligence Summaries are contained in F. S. Regs., Part II. and the Staff Manual respectively. Title pages will be prepared in manuscript.

| Place | Date | Hour | Summary of Events and Information | Remarks and references to Appendices |
|---|---|---|---|---|
| HERZEELE | 18th Aug | | Training carried out. Appendix "A" cancel order No 19 to be ready to move to PROVEN area | HSR 266 WI NN 62 |
| | 19th Aug | 12.5 pm | Operation order No 284 issued to move to PROVEN area. Summer drill moved out | APP (a) |
| PROVEN | 19th Aug | | 108 & 109 Bdes moved to PROVEN area in accordance with Bde order issued 11.30 am | |
| | Aug 20 | | Battalion carried out training in PROVEN area | |
| | 21st Aug | | 108 Lt Bde moved to Int reserve area at E.6.B.2.8. Sherford Park & fire line. 109 CHESHIRES REGT BROWN LINE | (3) MCLUSKIES 2nd Berkswood |
| | 22nd Aug | | Training carried out by the Battalions | |
| | 23rd Aug | | Training carried out by the Battalions | |
| | 24th Aug | | Operation order No 285 issued the relief of 117 Canadian Bn by 1/6 Cheshire Regt. Training carried out & Defence scheme reset round boundaries | APP D APP ? |

Army Form C. 2118.

# WAR DIARY
## or
## INTELLIGENCE SUMMARY.
(Erase heading not required.)

Instructions regarding War Diaries and Intelligence Summaries are contained in F.S. Regs., Part II and the Staff Manual respectively. Title pages will be prepared in manuscript.

| Place | Date | Hour | Summary of Events and Information | Remarks and references to Appendices |
|---|---|---|---|---|
| PROVEN | Aug 25th | | Enemy planes dropped bombs on HQ & 2 & HQ 58 | HERZEELE WINNEZEELE (1/40,000) |
| | Aug 26th | | Warning order received from Div re relief of 102nd Inf. Bde. By 14th Inf. Bde. Relieving policy. Appx for BOMB CAMP. 38th Divn. Operation order No 236 received re relief. | |
| | Aug 27th | | 102nd Bde relieved by 14th Inf. Bde & moved to Rail & ROAD CAMP. 1st JAN TER BIEZEN 102nd Inf. Bde. Order No 237 issued re move to CORMETTE CAMP. | APP (E) |
| CORMETTE | Aug 28th | 6.30 | 102nd Inf. Bde. moved to CORMETTE men by rail, transport by road. Bde. HQ units arrived and settled in new area. | HAZEBROUCK APP (F) |
| | Aug 29 | 2 am | Units transport arrived. Bde carried out training and schemes. | |
| | Aug 30 | | Pagers were kept all day carrying order of possible relief of 124 Bde. By B1. He 102nd Inf. Bde. | |

**Army Form C. 2118.**

# WAR DIARY
## or
## INTELLIGENCE SUMMARY.
(Erase heading not required.)

Instructions regarding War Diaries and Intelligence Summaries are contained in F. S. Regs., Part II. and the Staff Manual respectively. Title pages will be prepared in manuscript.

| Place | Date | Hour | Summary of Events and Information | Remarks and references to Appendices |
|---|---|---|---|---|
| CORBIE | Aug 30th | | Warning order issued to Bde that 123rd Bde may relieve 124th Inf. Bde. at ARBRE on night 1/2nd Sept. Battalions carried out training under Battalion arrangements. Casualties: Killed 5, Wounded 3, Missing — / Other Ranks: 17, 3, 2 / Edward Hilliam B.G. Gen. Commdg 123rd Inf. Bde. 123rd | 4/2/4 Bdds |

VOLUME XXXIII.

# APPENDICES
## FOR
# WAR DIARY
## 102ND INFANTRY BRIGADE H.Q.
## AUGUST - 1918

INFANTRY BRIGADE ORDER NO. 239

Ref. Map Sheet 28 S.W.

1. 102nd Infantry Brigade will be prepared to take over the whole of the Divisional front tonight btween the Divisional boundaries shewn on the map issued to Units under this Office B.M.A.1 today.

2. The 1/1st Hereford Regiment will take over the left sector irrespective of who is at present holding it. The front is at present held by the 101st Infantry Brigade.

3. The 1/7th Cheshire Regiment will take over the whole of the right sector. It is mainly held by the 103rd Infantry Brigade, but the 1/7th Cheshire Regiment will take over the whole front within the Brigade boundary.

4. Rhe 1/4th Cheshire Regiment will occupy the VIERSTRAAT SWITCH between the North and Southern Divisional boundaries.

5. The battalions will be organised in depth.

6. Immediate steps will be taken to reconoitre the lines and Units will first of all report to their respective Brigade Headquarters for guides.

7. The 102nd LT.M.B. will reconoitre the position held by the T.M. batteries of the 101st and 102nd Infantry Brigade and will be prepared to take over any of these positions.

8. "A" Coy M.G. Battalion will similarly reconoitre the positions of the M.G's of the 101st and 102nd Brigade and be prepared to take over any position.

9. Units will take immediate steps to ensure that communication is kept between them and their transports and make arrangements for all their requirements to be brought up before tonight.

10. Pack mules will be brought up and located under Lt. Wilson's arrangements. One pack mule from each Battalion will be sent to Brigade Headquarters for T.M.B work.

11. One limber of S.A.A. will also report to Brigade Headquarters from each Battalion. Immediately on relief tonight Units will get in touch with their flanks.

    1/1st Btn Herefords    Left. American Troops
                                        Right. 1/7th Btn Cheshire Regt.

    1/7th Btn Cheshires    Left. 1/1st Btn Hereford Regt.
                                        Right. British Troops.

ACKNOWLEDGE.

                                                (Sd) A.B. Leake Capt.
                                                    A/Brigade Major.
2/8/18.                                        102nd Infantry Brigade.

APPIA

Secret.
232    Copy No. 18

## 102nd Infantry Brigade Order No..

Ref. Maps
SOISSONS (1:100,000)(British).
OULCHY-LE-CHATEAU, 1:20,000.
BEAUVAIS   1/100,000

3rd Aug. 1918.

1. The Division is being withdrawn to the British zone.

2. The 102nd Infantry Brigade Group composed of units as under -

    102nd Infantry Brigade
    208th Field Co. R.E.
    "B" Coy. M.G. Battn.
    No. 3 Coy. Train.

    will move to the entrainment area as follows :-

    Dismounted personnel by bus in accordance with Table "A" attached.

    Mounted personnel by march route in accordance with Tables "B" and "C" attached, staging the night 4/5th instant in the NEUFCHELLES Area.

3. Transport of 102nd Infantry Brigade Group will march under orders of the Brigade Transport Officer.

4. Usual intervals will be observed by mounted and dismounted personnel on the line of march.

5. Staff Captain will issue instructions regarding Administrative arrangements.

6. Brigade Headquarters will close in the PARIS LINE at 8.0 a.m. on the 4th inst. and reopen in the new area at a time and place to be notified later.

7. Acknowledge (Members of 102 Bde. Group by bearer).

M. Carr Captain.
BRIGADE MAJOR.
102nd INFANTRY BRIGADE.

Distribution overleaf.

Distribution -

    102nd Inf. Bde. Order No.. ~~207~~ 232

---

    Copy No.1  G.O.C.
             2  Brigade Major
             3  Staff Captain
             4  Bde. Signal Officer.
             5  Bde. Transport Off.
             6  Bde. Intell. Off.
             7  Bde. Supply Off.
             8  No. 3 Coy. Train.
             9  "      M.G. Battn.
          10  208th Field Co. R.E.

          11  1/4th Cheshire Regt.
          12  1/7th Cheshire Regt.
          13  1/1st Bn Hereford Regt.
          14  101st Inf. Bde.
          15  103rd Inf. Bde.
          16  H.Q. 34th Div.

    17 & 18  ...  War Diary and File.

232

Table "A" - To accompany 102nd Infantry Brigade Order No.

Starting Point – Point where PARIS LINE cuts REUGNEUX—OULCHY-LE-CHATEAU Road.

| Ser. No. | Date | Unit (showing order of embusment.) | From | To | Time head of Units: column passes Starting Point. | ROUTE. | REMARKS. |
|---|---|---|---|---|---|---|---|
| 1. | 4.8.18. | 102nd Inf. Bde. H.Q. | Present location. | SILLY— LE-LONG— OGNES Area | 7.45 a.m. | Road junction just North of OULCHY LE CHATEAU — CHATEAU THIERRY—SOISSONS Road. | |
| 2. | -do- | 1/1st Bn. Hereford Regt. | -do- | -do- | 7.50 a.m. | -do- | |
| 3. | -do- | 1/4th Bn. Cheshire Regt. | -do- | -do- | 8.0 a.m. | -do- | |
| 4. | -do- | 1/7th Bn. Cheshire Regt. | -do- | -do- | Will proceed independently to embussing point. | GRAND ROZOY— OULCHY-LA-VILLE Road | Not to march on to main CHATEAU THIERRY—SOISSONS Road before 8.50 am |
| 5. | -do- | "B" Coy. M. G. Battn. | -do- | -do- | | -do- | -do- |
| 6. | -do- | 208th Field Co. R.E. No. 3 Coy. Train | -do- | -do- | | Any | -do- |

Time of embussing ..... 9.0 a.m.
Embussing Point ...... CHATEAU THIERRY — SOISSONS Road due East of BOIS DE LA BAILLETTE. (head of column 500x North of Point 139).
Debussing Point ...... Point in new area to be notified later.

TABLE "B"  To accompany 102nd Inf. Bde. Order No. ....

Starting Point ... Road Junction just N. of OULCHY LE VILLE.

| Ser. No. | Date | Unit | From | To | Time head of Units column passes Starting Point | Route | Remarks |
|---|---|---|---|---|---|---|---|
| 1. | 4.8.18 | Transport, 102nd Inf. Bde. H.Q. | Present location. | NEUFCHELLES BEAUVAL. | 9.30 a.m. | OULCHY-L.VILLE — PRINGY — NEUILLY — DAMMARD — MARGUIL — -SUR-OURCQ. | |
| 2. | -do- | Transport, 1/4th Bn. CHESHIRE REGT. | -do- | -do- | 9.33 a.m. | | |
| 3. | -do- | Transport, 1/7th Bn. CHESHIRE REGT. | -do- | -do- | 9.38 a.m. | | |
| 4. | -do- | Transport, 1/1st Bn. HEREFORD REGT. | -do- | -do- | 9.43 a.m. | | |
| 5. | -do- | Transport, "B" Co. M.G. Battalion. | -do- | -do- | 9.48 a.m. | | |
| 6. | -do- | Transport, 20th Field Co. R.E. | -do- | -do- | 10.0 a.m. | | |
| 7. | -do- | No. 3 Coy. Train. | -do- | -do- | 10.5 a.m. | | |

232

TABLE "C" — To accompany 102nd Inf. Bde. Order No... 201

Starting Point .. as selected by Off. i/c 102nd Bde. Group.

| Ser. No. | Date | Unit | From | To | ROUTE | Time head of Units column passes Starting Point. | REMARKS. |
|---|---|---|---|---|---|---|---|
| 1. | 5.8.18. | Transport, 102nd Inf. Bde. H.Q...... | NEUFCHELLES BEUVAL | CANES SILLY CHEVREVILLE | CUVERGNON —LEVIGNEN. | To be arranged by Bde.T.O. (R.A.Group starts at 6 am. followed by 105 & 101 Bde. Groups. | Units transports will be met at CHEVREVILLE where they will be notified of location of units. |
| 2. | -do- | Transport, 1/4th Bn. CHESHIRE REGT. | -do- | -do- | -do- | -do- | -do- |
| 3. | -do- | Transport, 1/7th Bn. CHESHIRE REGT. | -do- | -do- | -do- | -do- | -do- |
| 4. | -do- | Transport, 1/1st Bn. HEREFORD REGT. | -do- | -do- | -do- | -do- | -do- |
| 5. | -do- | Transport, "B" Co. M.G. Battalion.. | -do- | -do- | -do- | -do- | -do- |
| 6. | -do- | Transport, 208th Field Co. R.E... | -do- | -do- | -do- | -do- | -do- |
| 7. | -do- | No. 3 Coy. Train.. | -do- | -do- | -do- | -do- | -do- |

B.M.

102nd Brigade Administration Instructions No.

## 1. Advance Parties for Embussing.

The undermentioned Advance Parties will report to the Staff Captain on the Chateau THIERRY Rd. immediately E. of Point 129 - 1 Kilometre W. of GRAND ROZOY at 8-30 a.m. Infantry Battalions Offr 1, OR 3
Other Units — 1, 1

## 2. SUPPLIES

Rations for consumption August 5th must be carried by the men under Battalion arrangements to the Embussing Point, as no lorries or transport are available.

Supplies for consumption on 6th in the case of those units Embussing on the 5th will be drawn at the Embussing Station. In the case of those Embussing on the 6th they will be delivered on the 5th. Supplies for consumption on the 7th in the case of those Embussing on the 5th will be delivered in the new area by Supply Sections. In the case of those Embussing on the 6th. they will be drawn at the Embussing Station. Supplies for consumption on 8th will be delivered in the new area.

## 3. DETAILS

All details will rejoin their Units by 6 pm on the 4th the 4th inst. The following are the numbers for 102 Brigade.

1/4 Cheshire Rgt    8 - 133
1/7 Cheshire Rgt    12 - 127
1/1 Herfords Rgt    9 - 84
102nd L.T.M.B.      4 - 61

Details - Continued

Details will proceed retained up to and for the 5th

Greatcoats and Packs at strength shown below will be sent with details, and are in addition to those carried by them.

```
102nd Bde H.Q.        170
L.M.G Coy             145
1/4 Cheshire Regt     300
1/7 Cheshire Regt     520
1/1 Hereford Regt     360
```

4. Further details have been issued verbally to Quartermasters of each Battalion.

3/8/18.

A Bleath
Captain
Staff Captain
102nd Infantry Bde.

Secret.

APP. 16
232

Addendum to 102nd Infantry Brigade Order No.. ~~505~~.
_____

5th August, 1918.

1.     The Division will move by rail from the following stations :-

       ORMOY VILLERS - NANTEUIL - LE PLESSIS BELLEVILLE - DAMMARTIN -

2.     The 102nd Infantry Brigade Group will entrain in accordance with Table "D" attached.
       Units will move to entraining station under orders to be issued by Officers Commanding who will ensure arrival of units at the station at the times given.

3.     Lieut. SWALLOW attached Brigade Headquarters will superintend the entrainment.

4.     Advance parties of 1 Officer and 5 N.C.O's for Battalion and 1 Officer and 2 N.C.O's per other units will travel on the first train.
       Advance parties should bring horses or bicycles to enable them to proceed to their billeting areas on arrival.

5.     A loading party of 3 Officers & 100 other ranks will be found by the 1/1st Bn. Herefordshire Regt. and will report to the R.T.O. LE PLESSIS BELLEVILLE at 1.30 a.m. on the 6th instant. This party will be under the orders of the R.T.O. who will arrange accommodation. They will travel on the last train.

       An unloading party of 3 Officers and 100 other ranks will be found by the 1/7th Bn. Cheshire Regt. and will travel on the first train and will report to the R.T.O. at the detraining station immediately on arrival.

                                              6.. The ..

- 2 -

6.. The approximate duration of the journey will be 17 hours.
"Haltes repas" have been arranged at US - ACHERES (4 hours after departure) and at BOYELLES (10 hours after departure).

7.. Administrative instructions will be issued deparately.

8.. Acknowledge.

*M. Carr* Captain.
BRIGADE MAJOR.
102nd INFANTRY BRIGADE.

Distribution -

    G.O.C.
    Brigade Major
    Staff Captain.
    Signal Officer.
    Bde. Transport Officer.
    Bde. Gas Officer.
    Bde. Intell. Officer.
    1/4th Bn. Cheshire Regt.
    1/7th Bn. Cheshire Regt.
    1/1st Bn. Hereford Regt.
    208th Field Co. R.E.
    102nd L.T.M.B.
    "B" Coy. M.G. Battn.
    No. 3 Coy. Train
    34th Division.
    R.T.O. LE PLESSIS BELLAVILLE.

War Diary & File.

*******

Secret.                      102nd INFANTRY BDE.        T.S. 35/3 (APP 2)

Addendum No. 1
to
DEFENCE SCHEME - RESERVE BRIGADE - 34th DIV.

Reference Para. 5 -

1. **In event of attack - Main Hostile -**

(i)    "A" Battalion will at once move into BROWN Line South of Inter-Brigade boundary, still remaining in depth, and be prepared to move forward in a South-Easterly direction and deploy its front along the DICKEBUSH - BEEK Line and will form in depth 2 Companies forward in area H.18.a., B and c. one Company Support in H.12.d. and one Company Reserve BROWN Line. Battalion Headquarters with Reserve Company about H.12.c.

(ii)   "B" Battalion will at once occupy the ROME FARM Switch extending in posts from approximately POTTENHOEK FM (H.3.d.) in a North-Easterly direction through H.4.central to South-East corner B.28.d. then to BRIELEN defences. 3 Companies in Post line less 3 Platoons - 3 platoons in support (one platoon to each forward Company) and one Company in Reserve. O.C. Battalion with Reserve Company - and be prepared to move forward in a South-Easterly direction on the right of "A" Battalion and deploy in a similar manner as laid down for "A" Battalion in area H.17.c. and d., H.18.c. (front) and H.17.a. and b. (support) Reserve in BROWN Line H.11.c. and d.

(iii)   Dividing line between Battalions Road running North from H.18.c.5.8.

(iv)   "C" Battalion will remain in Reserve and occupy the GREEN Line North of Inter-Brigade boundary - disposed in depth 2 Companies front line - one support - one reserve - Battalion C.O. with Reserve Company.
In the event of the Brigade being ordered to move forward this Battalion will move into the BROWN Line South of Brigade boundary and remain in Reserve.

(v)   In event of above situation developing Brigade Headquarters remain in present position.

(vi)   This cancels para. 5 of Reserve Brigade Defence Scheme (T.S.35/3 dated 23.8.18) as far as 102nd Bde. is concerned.

Reference Para. 6 -

2. **In event of main hostile attack developing from North-East -**

(i)   "A" Battalion will occupy BROWN Line North of Inter-Brigade boundary H.5.b. and d. disposed in depth - 2 Companies in Front line, one support and one Coy. Reserve. O.C. Battalion with reserve, and if Brigade is ordered forward "A" Battalion will be prepared to move forward to KAAIE defences and deploy along the Line KAAIE - YPRES defences in area I.2.a. and c. making their Right Boundary about I.2.d.00.85, two Companies in Front, one Company Support, one Reserve. O.C.Battalion may if considered advisable be located in I.1.d. area.

"B" Battalion will occupy ROME FARM SWITCH as in para. 1 and will also be prepared to move forward in a similar manner as "A" Battalion, its Left in touch with 'A' Battalion's Right at I.2.d.00.85 deploying in areas I.2.c. and d. Two Companies

## Para. 2.(ii) continued.

in Front Line, one Company in Support, one Company in Reserve, O.C. Battalion with Reserve Company. Reserve Company may if considered necessary be located I.1.d. area.

(iii) "C" Battalion will occupy GREEN LINE North of Inter-brigade Boundary, two Companies in Front Line, one Company in Support, one Company in Reserve, O.C. Battalion with Reserve Company. In the event of Brigade being ordered forward, this Battalion will move forward and deploy in Area I.1.c. and I.7.a.

(iv) All Battalions will be prepared to move forward as may be ordered from above positions presumably in a N.E. direction.

(v) Brigade Headquarters if above situation arose would remain at G.6.a.2.4.

(vi) This cancels para. 6 in original scheme as far as 102nd Brigade is concerned.

3. ## Reference para. 7.

As detailed in original scheme.

4. O's. C. Battalions and Units will have all positions of assembly and routes to them and areas in front that they are liable to have to work over thoroughly reconnoitred by all concerned (O.C. Coys. Platoon Officers, N.C.O's and guides, all signallers, and any other unit that may be attached to them, Machine Gunners, Stokes Mortars.) They will also in conjunction with M.G. O.C. and Stokes Mortar O.C. select positions for each. O.C. forward Battalions will select routes to assembly positions in conjunction with each other so as to prevent crowding and confusion when moving. Battalions and Units must entirely rely on their own guides.

5. O.C. Signals will not be able to rely on lines so must establish communication by all means in their power.
O.C. Brigade Signals will establish forward relay stations as well as a report centre, these will be clearly shown on his disposition map and all concerned must be familiar with them.

6. Para. 8 of the Brigade Defence Scheme is very urgent.

7. O's. C. Battalions and Units of 102nd Infantry Brigade will send into Brigade Headquarters by first runner 25/8/1918 their schemes and dispositions in accordance with each phase of this Defence Scheme.

8. Map showing areas allotted to each Battalion in each Scheme attached.

9. ACKNOWLEDGE.

Edward Hill
Brigadier General,
COMMDG. 102ND INFANTRY BRIGADE.

24th August 1918.

---

Distribution: To all recipients of 102nd Infantry Brigade Defence Scheme.

Copy No 14

T.S.35/3

## DEFENCE SCHEME.
### RESERVE BRIGADE - 34th DIVISION.

Ref. Maps. -
Sheet 28 N.W. : 1/20,000

1. Divisional Reserve will consist of the Brigade of the 34th Division in Reserve (under the orders of the G.O.C., Reserve Brigade), the Reserve of the 43rd Brigade, 3 Field Companies R.E., and the 2/4th Bn. Somerset Light Infantry (Pioneers), and the 34th Bn. Machine Gun Corps (less 3 Companies).

2. The Division is responsible for fighting all lines from the FRONT SYSTEM to the YELLOW (BRANDHOEK) LINE inclusive, within the Divisional boundaries. These lines West of the Canal are -

   (a) DICKEBUSCH - GOLDFISH CHATEAU - BRIELEN LINE (BROWN LINE).
   Garrison - Two Battalions and 2 Sections M.Co.

   (b) OUDERDOM - VLAMERTINGHE - ELVERDINGHE Line (GREEN LINE).
   Garrison - One Brigade and one Company M.G.Battalion.
   Infantry disposed one battalion in each Sector with the third Battalion in reserve near ORILLA CAMP.

   (c) OUDERDOM - BRANDHOEK - WOESTEN LINE (YELLOW LINE).
   Garrison - One Brigade and one Company M.G.Battalion.

3. The present positions of the Reserve Brigade 34th Division and Reserve Battalion 43rd Brigade are :-

   Reserve Brigade "A" Battalion in BROWN LINE (H.5. and 6.)
   "B" Battalion in SIEGE CAMP (B.27.a.), just East of GREEN LINE.
   "C" Battalion in BRAKE CAMP (A.30.c.), behind the YELLOW LINE.

   Reserve Battalion 43rd Brigade 'B' Battalion in ORILLA CAMP (H.2.a.), behind the GREEN LINE.

4. There are three possible alternatives for hostile attack -

   (a) Main attack from S.E.
   (b) Main attack from N.E.
   (c) Direct frontal attack on MOOLE SPUR and YPRES - KAAIE Line.

   In either case the Reserve Brigade will be held in readiness to move with the object of forming in depth towards the threatened point.

5. If the main hostile attack is from the S.E. -

   (a) "A" Battalion will move to the BROWN LINE South of the Inter-Brigade boundary.

   "B" Battalion will occupy the ROME FARM SWITCH.

   "C" Battalion will occupy the GREEN LINE North of the Inter-Brigade boundary.

   "D" Battalion will occupy the GREEN LINE South of the Inter-Brigade boundary.

   "B" and "C" Battalions will be prepared to move forward to the BROWN LINE.

   (b) In this case......

5. continued. -

(b) In this case the Brigade consisting of "A", "B" and "C" Battalions if ordered to move would in the first instance be deployed on the line of DICKEBUSH BEEK with "A" on the Left, "B" Battalion in the Centre, "C" Battalion on the Right, and be prepared to attack in a Southerly or South-Easterly direction pivoting on the left.

6. If the main hostile attack develops from the N.E. -

(a) "A" Battalion will occupy the BROWN LINE North of the Inter-Brigade boundary.

(b) "B", "C" and "D" Battalions as in para. 5 (a).

(b) In this case the Brigade would, if ordered to move, assemble in the first instance in the KAAIE Defences, (I.2.a. and c.) and deploy on the line KAAIE - YPRES defences and prepare to move forward to the line of SAVILLE ROAD, approximately in line with GRID LINE running between Squares I.2. and I.3.

They will move to assembly positions in the KAAIE defences disposed as follows :-

"A" Battalion to right of KAAIE defences.
"B" Battalion Centre.
"C" Battalion to left.

On receipt of the order to deploy on the line KAAIE-YPRES defences, Battalions will move forward disposed as above.

7. If the main attack is a frontal one -

(a) "B" and "D" Battalions will occupy the GREEN LINE North and South of the Inter-Brigade boundaries respectively with "C" Battalion in reserve in the YELLOW LINE. "A" Battalion occupies the BROWN LINE.

(b) The subsequent movement of these Battalions would be either South-East or North-East as described in Paras. 5 & 6.

8. O's. C. Battalions as they occupy any of the positions allotted to the Reserve Brigade, 34th Division, will carry out the necessary reconnaisances to execute the movements indicated above.

9. R.E. and PIONEERS -

All personnel of R.E. Companies and the Pioneer Battalion out on working parties will return as follows -

(i) The Field Company in Right Brigade Sector to DRESSING Station which will be established in H.12.a. and there form part of the Reserve at the disposal of G.O.C. Right Brigade for R.E. services primarily to be used as Infantry only in extreme emergency.

(ii) The Field Company in the LEFT Brigade Sector to Company billets on CANAL BANK where they will be at the disposal of G.O.C. Left Brigade Sector for R.E. services primarily to be used as Infantry only in extreme emergency.

(iii) The two Pioneer Companies in the Forward Area will man that portion of the Support Line nearest to the Communication trench they may be working on. If not on work, these Coys. will be at the disposal of G.O.C. the Brigade in whose area they are quartered and will be used primarily in assisting to man the YPRES or KAAIE defences.

(IV) The......

Secret.

Addendum to 102nd Infantry Brigade Order No. 303.

5th August, 1918.

1. The Division will move by rail from the following stations :-

   ORMOY VILLERS - NANTEUIL - LE PLESSIS BELLEVILLE - DAMMARTIN -

2. The 102nd Infantry Brigade Group will entrain in accordance with Table "D" attached.
   Units will move to entraining station under orders to be issued by Officers Commanding who will ensure arrival of units at the station at the times given.

3. Lieut. SWALLOW attached Brigade Headquarters will superintend the entrainment.

4. Advance parties of 1 Officer and 5 N.C.O's for Battalion and 1 Officer and 2 N.C.O's per other units will travel on the first train.
   Advance parties should bring horses or bicycles to enable them to proceed to their billeting areas on arrival.

5. A loading party of 3 Officers & 100 other ranks will be found by the 1/1st Bn. Herefordshire Regt. and will report to the R.T.O. LE PLESSIS BELLEVILLE at 1.30 a.m. on the 6th instant. This party will be under the orders of the R.T.O. who will arrange accommodation. They will travel on the last train.

   An unloading party of 3 Officers and 100 other ranks will be found by the 1/7th Bn. Cheshire Regt. and will travel on the first train and will report to the R.T.O. at the detraining station immediately on arrival.

   6. The

- 2 -

6..     The approximate duration of the journey will be 17 hours.
        "Haltes repas" have been arranged at US - ACHERES (4 hours after departure) and at NOYELLES (10 hours after departure).

7..     Administrative instructions will be issued separately.

8..     Acknowledge.

*M. Carr*, Captain.
BRIGADE MAJOR.
102nd INFANTRY BRIGADE.

Distribution -

        G.O.C.
        Brigade Major
        Staff Captain.
        Signal Officer.
        Bde. Transport Officer.
        Bde. Gas Officer.
        Bde. Intell. Officer.
        1/4th Bn. Cheshire Regt.
        1/7th Bn. Cheshire Regt.
        1/1st Bn. Hereford Regt.
        208th Field Co. R.E.
        102nd L.T.M.B.
        "B" Coy. M. G. Battn.
        No. 3 Coy. Train
        34th Division.
        R.T.O. LE PLESSIS BELLEVILLE.

War Diary & File.

Table "D".  ENTRAINING TABLE to accompany 102nd Inf. Bde. Order No. 303 (Addendum).

Entraining Station .. LE PLESSIS BELLEVILLE.

| Ser. No. | Date | Unit | Time of arrival at entraining station. | Time of departure of train. | Detraining station. | Remarks. |
|---|---|---|---|---|---|---|
| 1. | 5.8.18 | Transport, 102nd Inf. Bde.H.Q. & Signal Section. "B" Coy. M.G. Battn | 2.0 a.m. | 6.9 a.m. | Not yet known. | |
| 2. | -do- | 102nd Inf. Bde. Hd. Qrs. Bde. Signal Section. 102nd L. T. M. Battery. "B" Coy. M. G. Battn. 100 O.R. 1/7th Ches. Regt. (unloading party) Advance parties all units. | 4.30 a.m. | 6.9 a.m. | -do- | |
| 3. | -do- | T'port, 1/4th Bn. Ches. Regt. | 6.0 a.m. | 10.9 a.m. | -do- | |
| 4. | -do- | 1/4th Bn. Cheshire Regt. | 8.30 a.m. | 10.9 a.m. | -do- | |
| 5. | -do- | T'port, 1/7th Bn. Cheshire Regt. | 10 a.m. | 2.9 p.m. | -do- | |
| 6. | -do- | 1/7th Bn. Ches. Regt. (less unloading party.) | 12.30 p.m. | 2.9 p.m. | -do- | |
| 7. | -do- | T'port, 1/1st Hereford Regt. | 2.0 p.m. | 6.9 p.m. | -do- | |
| 8. | -do- | 1/1st Bn. Hereford Regt. (less loading party) | 4.30 p.m. | 6.9 p.m. | -do- | |
| 9. | -do- | T'port, No. 5 Coy. Train T'port, 203th Field Co. R.E. | 6.0 p.m. | 10.9 p.m. | -do- | |
| 10. | -do- | No. 5 Coy. Train. 203th Field Co. R.E. Loading Party 1/1st Bn. Herefordshire Regt. | 8.30 p.m. | 10.9 p.m. | -do- | |

102nd Infantry Brigade Administrative Instructions No. 6.

1. **SUPPLIES.**

    Refilling Point for tomorrow and in future will be in ZEGGARS CAPPEL Village. *at 10 a.m.*

2. **STANDING ORDERS.**

    A copy of 2nd IInd Corps Town and Area Standing Orders is forwarded herewith. These Orders are to be brought to the notice of all ranks.

3. **FIRE.**

    It is very important that every precaution be made against fire and Fire Orders must be put up in every occupied billet. A copy of A.O./1 "Precautions against Fire" is forwarded for information.

4. **WATER.**

    The drinking water in the area is not good and Medical Officers must pay great attention to the chlorination of same. Water cart refilling points are as under:-

    | | |
    |---|---|
    | 1/1st Bn. Hereford Regt. | BOLLEZEELE. |
    | 1/4th Bn. Cheshire Regt. ) | |
    | 1/7th Bn. Cheshire Regt. ) | |
    | 102nd Field Ambulance. ) | LA CLOCHE. |
    | 208th Field Coy R.E. ) | |
    | No. 5 Coy. Train. ) | |

5. **CANTEEN.**

    The nearest E.F.C. is at WORMHOUDT.

6. **LEAVE.**

    Leave at the rate of 4 for:-

    1/4th Bn. Cheshire Regt.
    1/7th Bn. Cheshire Regt.
    1/1st Bn. Hereford Regt.

    commences tomorrow, August 9th. Personnel entrain at EBBLINGHEM at 8am on previous day. Personnel embarking 9th have already gone. Personnel embarking 10th entrain at EBBLINGHEM at 8am tomorrow, 9th August. Units should forward the names and particulars required two days in advance.

7. **LIBRARY.**

    There is a small library at the Area Commandant's Office, ZEGGARS CAPPEL. The Area Commandant will be pleased to loan any book he has on application.

8. **TRANSPORT.**

    The Brigade Commander has offered a prize for a Transport Competition to be held before the Brigade leave the present area - details will be issued in due course, but all units should at once begin to overhaul their transport and commence painting.

9. **PAINTING OF STEEL HELMETS.**

    The painting of steel helmets will be commenced forthwith.

10. **SPORTS.**

    There is a Tennis Court at Zeggars Cappel. *Particulars will be given on application to Staff Capt.*

    A.B.Beadle
    Captain,
    Staff Captain,
    102nd Infantry Brigade.

8/8/15.

## 102nd Brigade Administrative Instructions No. 6.

1. **SUPPLIES.**
Supplies for consumption tomorrow, 8th will be delivered this evening. Supplies for consumption, 7th will be drawn at the Entraining Station prior to departure and representatives of units should proceed with the Transport to take these over. Supplies for consumption 8th will travel on the wagons with units.

2. **ENTRAINMENT.**
   (a) All units will reconnoitre the route to the Entraining Station and ascertain the situation of forming up and watering places etc.
   (b) It is essential that the Entrainment of units be completed half an hour before the scheduled time of departure of the train, as the train will be moved from the entraining position at that hour.
   (c) Traffic Control Posts will be established in the approaches to the station. No troops will be allowed to enter the yard without first ascertaining that the R.T.O. is ready for them.
   (d) A complete Marching-Out State shewing the number of men, horses, G.S. and Limbered G.S. and 2 wheeled vehicles and Cycles should be sent down with the transport of each unit so that accommodation on the train can be checked by the R.T.O. at the beginning of the entrainment, Limbered G.S. Wagons being counted as 2 wheeled vehicles on the state.
   (e) Breast ropes for horse trucks must be provided by the units themselves, ropes for lashing vehicles in the flat trucks will be provided by the Railway.
   (f) All doors of the Covered Trucks and Carriages on the right hand side of the train when in the Main Line should be kept closed.
   (g) Supply and Baggage Wagons will accompany their own units in every case.

3. **DISCIPLINE.**
The Divisional Commander directs that great attention be paid to the orders as regards discipline during Moves by Train, which have already been issued. All ranks are to be warned that they are not permitted to leave the train without permission. Officers in Charge of train will ensure that steps are taken to take disciplinary action against any men who fail to observe this rule.

4. **LORRIES.**
5 lorries will report at the Church, SILLY-LE-LONG at 10am.
The undermentioned units must leave extra baggage behind to be picked up at 10am. They will each send a guide to the Church to take charge of one lorry.

       1/4th Bn. Cheshire Regt.
       102nd L.T.M.B.

The lorry of the L.T.M.B. on being loaded will proceed to 1/4th Bn. Cheshire Regt. to be filled up with any extra baggage of that Battalion.
The 3rd lorry will be for the 1/7th Bn Cheshire Regt who will send a guide at 10am also. This lorry may make a second journey.
The baggage of the 1/4th Bn. Cheshire Regt., and 102nd L.T.M.B. will be loaded on the train departing at 2-9pm.
The 1/1st Bn. Hereford Regt., will send 2 guides to be at the Church at 10am to remain with 2 of the lorries and to ensure that when these have completed the work of the L.T.M.B. and 1/4th Cheshire Regt., they return to 1/1st Hereford Regt for their baggage.

5/8/18

                                                    Captain.
                                                  Staff Captain.
                                        102nd Infantry Brigade.

Secret.  Copy No.. 14

## 102nd INFANTRY BRIGADE ORDER No.. 253

12 : 8 : 18

Ref. Maps -
Sheet 27 - 1:40,000.

1..     The 102nd Infantry Brigade will move to the HERZEELE Area to-morrow the 13th instant in accordance with Table "A" attached.

2..     Intervals as laid down in this office letter T.S. 67/1 dated 2nd July, 1918, will be observed on the line of march.  Units will halt at 10 minutes to the clock hour.
        Transport will march in rear of Units.
        Attention is called to this office letter T.S.67/5 dated 12.7.1918 with reference to order of march within Battalions.

3..     **Steel helmets will be carried on the back of the pack under the cross straps.**

4..     Instructions as to Advance parties, billet guides and Administrative arrangements will be issued by the Staff Captain.

5..     102nd Infantry Brigade Headquarters will close at ZEGGERS CAPPEL at 7.30 a.m. and re-open at HERZEELE at 8.30 a.m.

6..     Acknowledge.

M Carr  Captain.
BRIGADE MAJOR.
102nd INFANTRY BRIGADE.

102 B.H.Q.

Distribution -

        Copy No. 1  G.O.C.
             2  Brigade Major.
             3  Staff Captain.
             4  Bde. Supply Officer.
             5  Bde. Signal Officer.
             6  Bde. Intell. Officer.
             7  Bde. Gas Officer.
             8  Bde. Transport Officer.
             9  1/4th Bn Cheshire Regt.
            10  1/7th Bn Cheshire Regt.
            11  1/1st Bn Hereford Regt.
            12  102nd L.T.M.B.
            13  102nd Field Amb.
            14  No. 3 Coy. Train.
            15  54th Division.

        16 & 17  War Diary and File.

Table "A" - Accompanying 102nd Infantry Brigade Order No. 233

STARTING POINT — Point where Railway joins ZEGGERS CAPPEL — ESQUELBECQ Road just East of ZEGGERS CAPPEL. B.11.a.4.9. (Sheet 27).

| Ser. No. | UNIT. | From | To | Time head of Units column passes Starting Point. | ROUTE. | REMARKS. |
|---|---|---|---|---|---|---|
| 1. | 102nd Inf. Bde. H.Q. | ZEGGERS CAPPEL. | HERZEELE Area. | 7.45 a.m. | ESQUELBECQ WORMHOUDT. | |
| 2. | 102nd L.T.M. Bty. | -do- | -do- | 7.48 a.m. | -do- | |
| 3. | 1/4th Bn. Cheshire Regt. | -do- | -do- | 8.0 a.m. | -do- | |
| 4. | 1/7th Bn. Cheshire Regt. | -do- | -do- | 8.17 a.m. | -do- | |
| 5. | 1/1st Bn. Hereford Regt. | -do- | -do- | 8.34 a.m. | -do- | |
| 6. | No. 3 Coy. Train. | -do- | -do- | 9.0 a.m. | -do- | |

*War Diary* **APPIC**

AMENDMENT NO. 1 TO 102ND INFANTRY BRIGADE ORDER NO. 234
----------------

Table "B" issued with Addendum No. 3 to
Operation Order No. 234 is cancelled, and the attached
Table substituted.

Please acknowledge receipt.

*H L Carr* Captain.
BRIGADE MAJOR.
102nd INFANTRY BRIGADE.

Distribution as per
Brigade Order No. 234 - Add: No. 3.

SECRET.

Copy No..

## 102nd INFANTRY BRIGADE ORDER No... 234.

Ref. Maps –
Sheets 27 and 28
1:40,000.

18th Aug. 1918.

1.  The 34th Division is to relieve the 49th Division in the line.
    The 43rd Infantry Brigade (of the 14th Division) is at present attached to the 49th Division and will at the time of relief be holding the Right Brigade front.
    On completion of relief the 43rd Infantry Brigade with attached troops will come under the order of the G.O.C. 34th Division.

2.  The 102nd Infantry Brigade will move to the PROVEN AREA by march route on the 19th inst. in accordance with March Table "A" attached.
    On the 21st inst. the Brigade will move to the Reserve Area 49th Division in relief of the 146th Infantry Brigade. Detailed orders will be issued later.

3.  Usual distances will be observed on the line of march. Units will halt at 10 minutes to the clock hour. Transport will march in rear of units. Steel helmets will be carried on the back of the pack.

4.  Instructions with reference to advance parties, billet guides and administrative arrangements will be issued by the Staff Captain.

5.  Sector Commandants and guides in relief of similar parties of 147th Brigade will be detailed by Battalions as follows :-

|  | 1/4th Battn. Cheshire Regt. | | 1/7th Battn. Cheshire Regt. | | 1/1st Battn. Hereford Regt. | |
|---|---|---|---|---|---|---|
|  | N.C.O's. | Ptes. | Off. | Ptes. | Off. | Ptes. |
| GREEN LINE (VLAMERTINGHE) | – | 6 | 1 | 5 | – | 5 |
| YELLOW LINE (BRANDHOEK). | 1 | 6 | – | 6 | 1 | 5 |

Relief will be carried out on the 19th inst. Full details will be issued later.
Outgoing Commandants and guides will remain in their respective lines for 24 hours before relief.
All lines, dispositions, maps and schemes will be carefully taken over.

6.. 102nd Infantry Brigade Headquarters will close at HERZEELE at 7.30 a.m. on the 19th inst. and re-open in the PROVEN AREA at 8.30 a.m.

7.  Acknowledge.

M Carr Captain.
BRIGADE MAJOR.
102 B.H.Q.     102nd INFANTRY BRIGADE.

Distribution overleaf

102nd INFANTRY BRIGADE ORDER No. 234.

Ref. Maps.
Sheets 27 and 28
1:40,000.

16th Aug. 1916.

1. The 34th Division (now 102nd Division in the line).
The 102nd Infantry Brigade (of the 34th Division) is at present placed (or the 49th Division) at the disposition of relief by reliving the Black Watch front. On completion of relief the 102nd Infantry Brigade with attached troops will come under the order of the G.O.C. 34th Division.

2. The 102nd ......... will move to the FRONT AREA by ........ on the 19th inst. in accordance with march Table ........

Remainder of ............ will move to the ........ of the 102nd Infantry Brigade. Details ........ issued later.

3. ........ will be deployed on the line of march. Transport ........ to the joint Hours. ........ will be carried on ........ 2nd Brigade. Two ........ move .......... pending, Rifle guide and ........ arrangements will be issued by the .........

5. Either part 'a' of 102nd Brigade will be detailed by Battalions as follows :-

| | Lewis Guns. | 1/7th Battn. | 1/1st Battn. | Cheshire Regt. | Cheshire Regt. | Hereford Regt. |
|---|---|---|---|---|---|---|
| H.Q.O.'s. LEWIS. | 1 Off. | 1 Bns. | 1 Off. | 1 N.C.O. |
| FRONT LINE (WARNIMONT) | | | 3 | | 7 | 5 |
| SUPPORT LINE (HUMBERT). | | 3 | 3 | 6 | 7 | 8 |

Relief will be carried out on the 19th inst. Full details will be issued later.
Outgoing Coy anchors and Guides will remain in their respective lines for 48 hours before relief.
All Maps, dispositions, maps and sconces will be carefully taken over.

6. 102nd Infantry Brigade Headquarters will close at HERISSARD at 7.30 a.m. on the 19th inst. and re-open in the PROVEN AREA at 5.30 p.m.

7. Acknowledge.

M.G. .......... Captain.
BRIGADE MAJOR.
for B.M. 102nd INFANTRY BRIGADE.

Distribution overleaf.

March Table "A"    To accompany 102nd Infantry Brigade Order No. 234

Starting Point - Cross Roads 500X East of HERZEELE D.10.d.1.3.

| Ser. No. | Date | Unit | From | To | Time head of Units column passes Starting Point. | Route | REMARKS. |
|---|---|---|---|---|---|---|---|
| 1. | 19.8.18 | 102nd Infantry Brigade H.Q. | HERZEELE Area. | PROVEN Area. | 8.0 a.m. | HERZEELE - HOUTKERQUE E.21.b.1.7. E.15.b.8.2. | |
| 2. | -do- | 102nd L.T.M. Battery | -do- | -do- | 8.3 a.m. | -do- | |
| 3. | -do- | 1/1st Battn. Hereford Regt. | -do- | -do- | 8.5 a.m. | -do- | |
| 4. | -do- | 1/4th Battn. Cheshire Regt. | -do- | -do- | 8.22 a.m. | -do- | |
| 5. | -do- | 1/7th Battn. Cheshire Regt. | -do- | -do- | 8.39 a.m. | -do- | Will halt while passing Starting Point. |
| 6. | -do- | No. 5 Coy. Train. | -do- | -do- | 9.3 a.m. | -do- | |
| 7. | 21.8.1918 | 102nd Inf. Bde. | PROVEN AREA. | RESERVE AREA 49th DIVISION. | - | - | In relief of 148th Inf. Bde. Details later. |

TABLE "B" - to accompany 102nd Inf. Bde. Order No. 234 (Add. No. 5 - Amendt. No.1)

Starting Point ... Cross Roads F.21.a.2.6. (Sheet 27)

| Ser. No. | Date | Unit | From | To | In relief of | Time head of Units col. passes S. Pt. | Route |
|---|---|---|---|---|---|---|---|
| 1. | 21.8.18. | 1/1st Battn. Herefordshire Regt. | PIGEON CAMP. | SIEGE CAMP. | 1/4th Battn. K.O.Y.L.I. | 10.0 a.m. | PROVEN-POPERINGHE Road - F.21.a.2.6. - New straight road to INTERNATIONAL CORNER A.9.c.2.5. - A.29.Central. |
| 2. | -do- | 1/4th Bn. Cheshire Regiment. | PENTON CAMP. | BRAKE CAMP. | 1/4th Batt. Yorks.& Lancs. | 10-40 a.m. | |
| 3. | -do- | 102nd Inf. Bde. Hd. Qrs. | PROVEN. | BRAKE CAMP. | 148th Inf. Bde. H.Q. | 11-25 a.m. | |
| 4. | -do- | 102nd L.T.M.B. | PROVEN. | BRAKE CAMP. | 148th L.T.M.B. | 11-30 a.m. | |
| 5. | -do- | 1/7th Battn. Cheshire Regt. | PEKIN CAMP. | BROWN LINE. | 1/5th Batt. Yorks.& Lancs. | 11-55 a.m. | |
| 6. | -do- | (*) T'port Bde. H.Q. & 102nd L.T.M.B. | PROVEN. | A.30. | - | 12-20 a.m. | |
| 7. | -do- | T'port 1/1st Bn. Hereford Regt. | PIGEON CAMP. | A.30. | - | 12-25 p.m. | |
| 8. | -do- | (*) T'port 1/4th Bn. Cheshire Regt. | PENTON CAMP. | A.30 | - | 12-30 p.m. | |

P.T.O.

TOBALE

TABLE "B" (Continued)

| | | | | | |
|---|---|---|---|---|---|
| 9. | 21-3-18.(*) | T'port 1/7th Bn.Cheshire Rgt. | PLAIN CAMP. | A.30. | 12-35 p.m. |
| 10. | -do- | (*) No. 3 Coy.Train. | PROVEN. | A.5.&.8.5. | 12-40 p.m. |

Note. (*) Incoming transport will give way to outgoing troops - 100 yds. to be maintained between every 6 vehicles.

P.T.O.

Copy No.......

ADDENDUM NO. 2 to 102ND INFANTRY BRIGADE ORDER NO. 234.

1. Battalions of the 102nd Infantry Brigade will relieve Battalions of the 146th Infantry Brigade on 21st instant as follows :-

   1/7th Bn. Cheshire Regt. will relieve 5th Bn. Yorks. & Lancs.
   Regiment in the BROWN LINE.

   1/1st Bn. Hereford Regt. will relieve the 4th Bn. K.O.Y.L.I.,
   at SIEGE CAMP (B.27.a.)

   1/4th Bn. Cheshire Regt. will relieve 4th Bn. Yorks. & Lancs.
   Regiment at BRAKE CAMP (A.30.c.)

   Detailed March Orders will follow later.

2. The following advance parties will report at the Headquarters of the 146th Infantry Brigade, BRAKE CAMP, at 4 p.m. on the 20th instant.

   2 Officers per Battalion.
   1 N.C.O. per Company.
   1 N.C.O. per Transport.
   1 Officer and 1 N.C.O. per T.M.B.

   These parties will remain with outgoing Battalions the night of 20th/21st, and will rejoin their Units on arrival.

3. The Commanding Officer and Adjutant of the 1/7th Bn. Cheshire Regiment will arrange to carry out a reconnaisance of the BROWN LINE on the 20th instant. Full details of regarding the line can be obtained from 146th Infantry Brigade Headquarters, BRAKE CAMP.

M. Carr  Captain,
                Brigade Major,
                102nd Infantry Brigade.

19/6/1918.

Distribution as per Brigade Order No. 234.

Copy to 148th Inf Bde

Addendum No. 1
to
102nd Infantry Brigade Order No... 234

\*:\*:\*:\*:\*

18 : 8 : 1918.

With reference to para. 5 of Brigade Order No. 234 -

1.. **GREEN LINE (VLAMERTINGHE)** -

    The six and five privates of the 1/4th Bn. Cheshire Regt. and 1/1st Bn. Herefordshire Regt. respectively will report on the 19th inst. to the Officer-i-c- at the Headquarters of the 1/7th Bn. Cheshire Regt. immediately on the arrival of the Brigade in the PROVEN AREA tomorrow.

    The Headquarters of the Sector Commandant, GREEN LINE, is at ORILLIA CAMP, H.3.a.7.9. (Sheet 28).

    O.C. 1/7th Bn. Cheshire Regt. will please arrange the necessary transport for Officers baggage and men's packs.

2.. **YELLOW LINE (BRANDHOEK)** -

    The 1 N.C.O. and 6 privates 1/4th Bn. Cheshire Regt. and 6 privates of the 1/7th Bn. Cheshire Regt. will report to the Officer i/c at the Headquarters of the 1/1st Bn. Herefordshire Regt. on the 19th inst. immediately on arrival of the Brigade in the PROVEN AREA.

    The Headquarters of the Sector Commandant, YELLOW LINE, is at BRAKE CAMP, A.30.c.8.3. (Sheet 28)

    O.C. 1/1st Bn. Herefordshire Regt. will please arrange transport for Officers baggage and men's packs.

3.. The Sector Commandants will march off their parties as soon as they are assembled. Completion of relief will be reported to Bde.H.Q. PROVEN.

18:8:1918.

                      Captain.
                BRIGADE MAJOR
Distribution -     102nd INFANTRY BRIGADE.

As per O.O. No. 234.

\*:\*:\*

B.M.

Amendment to 102nd Brigade Administrative Instructions No. 9.

Reference Paragraph 2.

If it is not possible to obtain lorries, 6 G.S. Wagons (2 for each Battalion) will report at the Square, HERZEELE at 6.30 a.m., where Guides will meet them.

*[signature]*
Captain.
Staff Captain.
102nd Infantry Brigade.

18/8/18.

## 102nd Brigade Administrative Instructions No. 9.

1. **SUPPLIES.**
Supplies for consumption 20th instant are being dumped in the new area today. Refilling will take place by Train Wagons at 9-30am tomorrow, August 19th and until further notice at E.12.d.3.8.

2. **BAGGAGE.**
½ lorry will be at the disposal of each Battalion for conveyance of extra baggage. The attention of all units is once again drawn the importance of reducing the amount of extra baggage to the absolute minimum. The possibility of obtaining lorries is never a certainty and unless units make a special effort to ensure that no unnecessary baggage is carried it may found at some future time that some of it is unavoidably left behind.

The lorries will report at the Square HERZEELE at 6-45am. Guides from the 1/4th and 1/7th Bns. Cheshire Regt. will meet one and Guides from the 1/1st Bn. Hereford Regt. and Brigade Hqrs will meet the other. The 1/4th Bn. Cheshire Regt. and 1/1st Bn. Hereford Regt. will half load first. Lorries will not be allowed to make a double journey.

3. **ADVANCED PARTIES.**
Advance Parties as under will report to the Area Commandant PROVEN at 4-30pm today.

| | |
|---|---|
| Infantry Battalions | 2 Officers. |
| | 1 N.C.O. per Coy. |
| | 1 N.C.O. or man per Platoon. |
| | 1 N.C.O. for Transport. |
| Other Units. | 1 Offr. & 1 N.C.O. |

Units will be responsible for arranging for their own Guides to meet them tomorrow.

4. **BILLETS & AREA STORES.**
Units must ensure that their Billetting Certificates are handed in to the Maire before leaving. All Units will render a certificate to Brigade Hqrs. by 7am tomorrow that this had been done and also to the effect that all billets have been left in a clean and sanitary condition.

Any tents, stores, etc. borrowed from the Area Commandant will be returned by 7am tomorrow.

5. **MEDICAL ARRANGEMENTS.**
From noon today the 102nd Field Ambulance is responsible for the collection of Sick of the 102nd Infantry Brigade.
Location of 102nd Field Ambulance is LISTER CAMP, W.23.a.3.8. (Sheet 19). On the HAZEBROUCK 5A Map - ¼ inch S.W. of H in ROUSBRUGGE-HARINGHE, 1.H.5.0.

6. **MARCHING IN STATE.**
All units will render to Brigade Headquarters by 6pm tomorrow, a Marching-in State into the new area.

Captain.
Staff Captain.
102nd Infantry Brigade.

18/8/18.

SECRET.

PROVISIONAL DEFENCE SCHEME.
RESERVE BRIGADE.

1. The Reserve Brigade will be disposed with one Battalion in the BROWN LINE, North of the Inter-Brigade Boundary, and having one Company forward in I.1.a., one Battalion at CHINE CAMP, one Battalion at BRAKE CAMP.

2. In the event of a hostile attack from any direction the CHINE CAMP Battalion will occupy the GREEN LINE, North of the Inter-Brigade Boundary, and the BRAKE CAMP Battalion the GREEN LINE South of the Inter-Brigade Boundary, within the Divisional Area.

3. Both Battalions in the GREEN LINE and the forward Battalion will be held in readiness to move to the threatened flank if required.

4. Cross country tracks for the assembly about H.19.a. and B. of the Battalion in the BROWN LINE and its detached Company in I.1.a., in the event of the Southern flank of the Division being threatened will be reconnoitred by the Battalions holding the BROWN LINE.

5. Positions are shown on Map 'A' attached.

          Captain,
          Brigade Major,
        102ND INFANTRY BRIGADE.

21/8/1918.


To O's. C.,
 1/4th Bn. Cheshire Regiment.
 1/7th Bn. Cheshire Regiment.
 1/1st Bn. Hereford Regiment.
 34th Division "G" (for information).

Forwarded for information and necessary action.

Please acknowledge.

          Captain,
          Brigade Maj
        102ND INFANTRY BRIGADE.

21/8/1918.

Copy No...6...

ADDENDUM NO. 2 to 102ND INFANTRY BRIGADE ORDER NO. 234.

1. Battalions of the 102nd Infantry Brigade will relieve Battalions of the 148th Infantry Brigade on 21st instant as follows :-

   1/7th Bn. Cheshire Regt. will relieve 5th Bn. Yorks. & Lancs. Regiment in the BROWN LINE.

   1/1st Bn. Hereford Regt. will relieve the 4th Bn. K.O.Y.L.I., at SIEGE CAMP (B.27.a.)

   1/4th Bn. Cheshire Regt. will relieve 4th Bn. Yorks. & Lancs. Regiment at BRAKE CAMP (A.30.c.)

   Detailed March Orders will follow later.

2. The following advance parties will report at the Headquarters of the 148th Infantry Brigade, BRAKE CAMP, at 4 p.m. on the 20th instant.

   2 Officers per Battalion.
   1 N.C.O. per Company.
   1 N.C.O. per Transport.
   1 Officer and 1 N.C.O. per T.M.B.

   These parties will remain with outgoing Battalions the night of 20th/21st, and will rejoin their Units on arrival.

3. The Commanding Officer and Adjutant of the 1/7th Bn. Cheshire Regiment will arrange to carry out a reconnaissance of the BROWN LINE on the 20th instant. Full details of regarding the line can be obtained from 148th Infantry Brigade Headquarters, BRAKE CAMP.

*M. Carr*
Captain,
Brigade Major,
102nd Infantry Brigade.

19/8/1918.

Distribution as per Brigade Order No. 234.

Copy to 148 Inf Bde -

**Secret.**

102nd Infantry Brigade Order No. 235

Copy No. 4

Ref. Map -
Sheet 28 N.W. - 1:20,000.

1. The 1/4th Bn. Cheshire Regt. will relieve the 1/7th Bn. Cheshire Regt. in the Reserve Forward Area on the 26th inst.

2. On relief the 1/7th Bn. Cheshire Regt. will occupy the area vacated by 1/4th Bn Cheshire Regt.

3. The relief will be carried out in daylight and to be completed by 4.0 p.m.

4. Both Battalions will move by Sections only.

5. O.C. Battalions will please see that the clearest possible orders are given to Section Commanders that they are acquainted with the routes to be followed.

6. Battalion Commanders must be responsible that good distances are kept and that Sections move as much under cover as possible both in-coming and out-going.

7. All arrangements re. relief will be made by Battalion Commanders. The Battalion moving forward will take up positions already occupied by Battalion now forward.

8. The usual forward or advanced parties will be sent forward.

9. Officers Commanding Battalions will exchange their Defence Schemes in accordance with Brigade Defence Scheme.

10. The 1/1st Bn. Herefordshire Regt. will not move.

11. The 1/1st Bn. Herefordshire Regt. will find all R.E. work parties that are detailed for the 26.8.1918, both 1/7th Cheshire Regt. and 1/4th Cheshire Regt., and the O.C. will ensure that all his necessary guides &c. are arranged so as to ensure that the work is carried out without any delay. He will get in touch with 1/4th Cheshire Regt. and 1/7th Cheshire Regt. for all particulars.

12. Officers Commanding Battalions will report relief complete by code word "SPOT" and time.

13. Acknowledge.

Edward Hilliam
Brigadier-General.
Commanding 102nd Infantry Brigade.

Distribution -

Copy No. 1 G.O.C.
2 Staff Captain.
3 Bde. Transport Off.
4 Bde. Intell. Off.
5 Bde. Signal Officer.
6 1/4th Cheshire Regt.
7 1/7th Cheshire Regt.
8 1/1st Hereford Regt.
9 102nd L.T.M.B.
10 Bde. Supply Officer.
11 No. 3 Coy. Train.
12 101st Inf. Bde.
13 103rd Inf. Bde.
14 34th Div.
15 12th Belgian Div.
16 104th Fld. Amb.

17 & 18 .. War Diary & File.

*War Diary*

## 102nd Infantry Brigade Order No. 235

Secret.                                                                  Copy No. 17.

Ref. Map -
Sheet 28 N.W. - 1:20,000.

1. The 1/4th Bn. Cheshire Regt. will relieve the 1/7th Bn. Cheshire Regt. in the Reserve Forward Area on the 26th inst.

2. On relief the 1/7th Bn. Cheshire Regt. will occupy the area vacated by 1/4th Bn Cheshire Regt.

3. The relief will be carried out in daylight and to be completed by 4.0 p.m.

4. Both Battalions will move by Sections only.

5. O.C. Battalions will please see that the clearest possible orders are given to Section Commanders that they are acquainted with the routes to be followed.

6. Battalion Commanders must be responsible that good distances are kept and that Sections move as much under cover as possible both in-coming and out-going.

7. All arrangements re. relief will be made by Battalion Commanders. The Battalion moving forward will take up positions already occupied by Battalion now forward.

8. The usual forward or advanced parties will be sent forward.

9. Officers Commanding Battalions will exchange their Defence Schemes in accordance with Brigade Defence Scheme.

10. The 1/1st Bn. Herefordshire Regt. will not move.

11. The 1/1st Bn. Herefordshire Regt. will find all R.E. work parties that are detailed for the 26.8.1918, both 1/7th Cheshire Regt. and 1/4th Cheshire Regt., and the O.C. will ensure that all his necessary guides &c. are arranged so as to ensure that the work is carried out without any delay. He will get in touch with 1/4th Cheshire Regt. and 1/7th Cheshire Regt. for all particulars.

12. Officers Commanding Battalions will report relief complete by code word "SPOT" and time.

13. Acknowledge.

*Edward Hilliam*
Brigadier-General.
Commanding 102nd Infantry Brigade.

Distribution -

Copy No. 1 G.O.C.
         2 Staff Captain.
         3 Bde. Transport Off.
         4 Bde. Intell. Off.
         5 Bde. Signal Officer.
         6 1/4th Cheshire Regt.
         7 1/7th Cheshire Regt.
         8 1/1st Hereford Regt.
         9 102nd L.T.M.B.
        10 Bde. Supply Officer.
        11 No. 3 Coy. Train.
        12 101st Inf. Bde.
        13 103rd Inf. Bde.
        14 34th Div.
        15 12th Belgian Div.
        16 104th Fld. Amb.
        17 & 18 .. War Diary & File.

Addendum No. 3
to
102nd Infantry Brigade Order No. 234

20th Aug. 1918.

1. The 102nd Infantry Brigade will relieve the 148th Infantry Brigade in accordance with Table "B" attached.

2. Steel helmets will be worn and Box Respirators in the Alert position. All movement along and East of the PROVEN--POPERINGHE Road will be by platoons at 100$^x$ distance. East of VLAMERTINGHE all movement will be by Sections at 100$^x$ distance.

3. Guides provided by 148th Infantry Brigade will meet Units at road junctions, A.30.central, BRAKE CAMP, as follows :-

    1 guide per Battalion Headquarters.
    1 guide  " Company Headquarters.
    1 guide  " Platoon.

4.. O's. C. Battalions will arrange for a reconnaisance of the route to be carried out before the march.

5.. Transport will be brigaded and will march under the orders of the Brigade Transport Officer except Lewis Gun Limbers of all Battalions and Cookers, Mess and Officers Baggage wagon of 1/1st Bn. Herefordshire Regt. which will march with Battalions.

6.. Staff Captain will issue instructions regarding Administrative arrangements.

7.. 102nd Infantry Brigade Headquarters will close at PROVEN at 4.0 p.m. and re-open at BRAKE CAMP at the same hour.

8.. Acknowledge.

M Carr Captain.
BRIGADE MAJOR.
102nd INFANTRY BRIGADE.

Distribution as per
    Brigade Order No. 234 -

        Copies to - 148th Inf. Bde.
                    49th Division.
                    Off. i/c Bde. School.

File G.O.C.

## 102nd Infantry Brigade Administrative Instructions No.10.

To accompany 102nd Brigade Order No. 234 Addendum No.3.

1. **SUPPLIES.** Supplies for consumption 22nd will be refilled at 9-30am tomorrow at the present Refilling Point. Supply wagons will join and march with units to the new area. Supplies for consumption 23rd will be refilled at A.28.a.8.3. Sheet 28, on the 22nd. From a date which will be notified later Supplies will be drawn from Railhead by Horse Transport and from Refilling Point by First Line Transport. One complete day's preserved rations will be held by M.T.Coy and units will be fed direct from Railhead.

2. **BAGGAGE.** One G.S. Wagon will be at the disposal of each Battalion tomorrow for extra baggage and units will each send a guide to Brigade Headquarters at 10am to meet these.

3. Units will send the usual certificate of cleanliness of Camp to Brigade Headquarters at 11-30am tomorrow and will forward a Marching in State into the new area as usual.

4. **MEDICAL ARRANGEMENTS.** A Horsed Ambulance will follow in rear of the Column and carry men falling out who are unable to march further will wait until picked up. The Ambulance will proceed to BRAKE CAMP- to the Headquarters of the 104th Field Ambulance.
   The Headquarters of the 104th Field Ambulance who will carry out the clearing of the Forward Area is at A.30.central.
   A copy of Medical Arrangements (Active) No. 55 - 34th Division is forwarded herewith (to Battalions only) and Medical Officers will take the first opportunity of reconnoitring the Forward Area and making themselves acquainted with these arrangements. They apply not only to the Reserve Area, but also to the Forward Area.

5. A copy of 34th Div. Administrative Instructions No. 59 is also enclosed (to Battalions) showing :-
   1. Locations.
   2. Transport Lines.
   3. Ammunition Supply.
   4. Supplies.
   5. Light Railways.
   6. R.E. Supplies.
   7. Water Supply.
   8. Baths.
   9. Solder.
   10. Salvage.
   11. Cemeteries.
   12. Traffic.
   13. Miscellaneous.
   
   A great deal of the above applies to the Forward Area (other than Reserve Brigade) and units should take every opportunity of familiarising themselves with these Administrative arrangements.

6. **STORES.** Receipts for all Stores, both Trench and Area, which have been taken over by Advance Parties will be forwarded to Brigade H.Q. by 9am, August 22nd.

A.B.L. Eakle
Captain.
Staff Captain.
102nd Infantry Brigade.

20/8/18.

T.O. 35/9

1/4th Bn. Cheshire Regt.
1/7th Bn. Cheshire Regt.
1/1st Bn. Hereford Regt.

        The enclosed copy of 58th Div. Defence Instructions No.4.- DEMOLITIONS is to be attached to Reserve Brigade Defence Scheme, issued by this Office.

                                    for,
                                 Brigade Major,
                         102nd Infantry Brigade.

23/3/18.

COPY.

# 34th DIVISION.
## Defence Instructions No.4.
### DEMOLITIONS.

SECRET
Copy No.5.

1. The prepared demolitions are divided into three groups :-
   A. Forward Group  }
   B. Centre    "    }  Lists attached.
   C. Rear      "    }

   Of these, the forward group are all in front of the Brown or SHIELKA Line.
   The Centre Group are all in front of the Green or VLAMERTINGE Line.
   The rear Group are all behind the Green Line.

2. SCHEME FOR FIRING "A" Group.
   (a) 1 R.E. Officer belonging to the left Field Coy, together with two detachments of R.E. - one from each of the two Field Coys. in the line - have been detailed permanently to furnish a Guard of 2 R.E. for each prepared charge. The Officer will live with the Right Battalion H.Q. of the Left Brigade in the Ramparts. The detachments will be of such strength as to allow 2 sappers to each charge, except that on WELL CROSS ROADS, which will have one Lance-Corporal and two sappers. It is the duty of the Officer and detachments to patrol daily all the charges and see that they are efficient and ready for being fired.

   (b) The charges will be fired as follows :-
   Nos. 2,3,4,7,&9 by order from Divisional Headquarters on commencement of bombardment preceding an expected attack, or if the attack is a surprise or not preceded by a bombardment, by order of O.C. Right Battalion, Left Brigade. The charges will be blown as soon as it is reasonably certain an attack is imminent as the routes they destroy are not intended to serve any tactical purpose for own troops. The remainder of the charges in Group "A" with the exception of the charge at WELLS CROSS ROADS I.2.d.1.7. will be blown by the guards as soon as they observe the ascent of 2 rockets with GREEN PARACHUTE LIGHT, from the MACHINE GUN SIDING H.19.a.8.8. These rockets will be fired by O.C. Field Coy., R.E. in the Right Sector when he observes a similar pair of rockets fired from H.Q. of LEFT BRIGADE. These rockets will be fired on the responsibility of the G.O.C. LEFT BRIGADE after consultation with D.H.Q. or if communication is interrupted on his own responsibility.
   The charge at WELLS CROSS ROADS I.2.d.1.7. will be fired by order of the O.C. Reserve Battn. Left Brigade after it appears to him probable that the enemy will gain possession of the cross Roads and after the men have been withdrawn to a safe distance, i.e. 200 yards. For this purpose a Lce. Cpl. R.E. will be attached to O.C. Reserve Battn. Left Brigade in addition to 2 R.Es. as guard to the charge.

3. SCHEME FOR FIRING GROUPS "B" & "C".
   One Officer and a patrol will be detailed permanently from the Field Coy. in reserve (Divisional) to visit and keep charges efficient.
   On the order "Prepare to fire" Group "B" or "C" being passed to O.C. Reserve Field Coy., he will detail sufficient R.E. to allow of two sappers to each charge in the group concerned. This detachment will be dispatched by the Officer with the Reserve Brigade to the various charges on receiving the order from Div. H.Q. to fire any or all of the charges.

                                                    Sgd.     x    x
                                                    Lieut Col. G.S.
                                                    34th Division.

23/8/18.

DISTRIBUTION :- as per defence instructions Nos. 2 & 3.

                                                    Lists A. B. & C on reverse.

## LIST "A" - FORWARD GROUP.

| No. | Bridges etc. | Location. | R.E.Fld.Coy. responsible. |
|---|---|---|---|
| 1. | HELL CROSS ROADS | I.2.d.1.7. | Left Coy. |
| 2. | Cross Roads at - | I.9.b.5.9. | " " |
| 3. | YPRES MOAT - MENIN GATE. | I.8.b.8.1. | " " |
| 4. | LILLE GATE CAUSEWAY, YPRES MOAT. | I.14.a.3.6. | Right " |
| 5. | CAUSEWAY Plank Road. | I.13.b.9.4. | " " |
| 6. | YPRES-COMINES CANAL, DICKEBUSCH-YPRES Rd. | I.13.a.7.4. | " " |
| 7. | YPRES-COMINES CANAL, VLAM-YPRES Road. | I.7.c.6.7. | " " |
| 8. | YPRES-COMINES CANAL, BEDFORD Road. | I.7.a.7.6. | Left " |
| 9. | YPRES-COMINES CANAL, Artillery Bridge. | I.7.b.2.9. | " " |
| 10. | YPRES-COMINES CANAL, Lock 12. | I.1.d.3.9. | " " |
| 11. | YPRES-COMINES CANAL, Bridge. | I.1.c.4.9. | " " |
| 12. | Lock No. 13. | I.1.b.7.1. | " " |
| 13. | Cross Roads at - | C.1.c.1.6. | " " |
| 14. | Trees at - | H.12.c.3.5. | Right " |

## LIST "B" - CENTRE GROUP.

| 1. | Railway Bridge. | H.9.c.4.6. |
|---|---|---|
| 2. | Brick Culvert. | H.4.a.9.7. |
| 3. | Railway Bridge. | H.10.b.1.1. |
| 4. | Road Bridge. | H.9.a.3.8. |
| 5. | Culvert under Road. | H.3.d.4.2. |
| 6. | MARSH FARM Road, Wooden Road Bridge. | H.2.a.7.7. |
| 7. | Wooden Road Bridge over KEMMELBEEK. | H.3.d.1.4. |
| 8. | Light Railway Bridge. | B.27.c.3.3. |
| 9. | Farm Road Bridge. | B.27.c.4.1. |

## LIST "C" - REAR GROUP.

| 1. | BRANDHOEK CROSS Roads. | G.23.d.3.0. |
|---|---|---|
| 2. | Trees (7) | G.4.c.0.1. |
| 3. | Railway Bridge. | G.10.b.5.9. |
| 4. | Road Bridge over ROBART BEEK. | G.4.d.35.35. |

Extract -

## BATTALION SIGNAL OFFICER.

1. **Proceeding into the line** -

(a) He will obtain a diagram of the Battalion Communications in existence, and enter them on a map, a copy of which, when he has verified it, he will forward to the Brigade Signal Section Officer.

(b) He will proceed round the Battalion Communications with the outgoing Battalion Signal Officer.

(c) He, will on being informed by the Brigade Signal Section Officer of the position of Visual, wireless, amplifier and power buzzer, stations, see that all Officers in his Battalion are made acquainted as soon as possible with these locations and with whom they are in communication.

2. **Whilst holding the line.** -

(a) He will daily go round the Battalion system of communications, and see that they are working satisfactorily. He will report at least once a day by wire or telephone to the Brigade Signal Section Officer on the state of his communications.

2a. **Pigeons.** Battalion Signal Officers will see that the pigeons allotted to them are released within 24 hours. Birds in the assault pigeon baskets get cramped, and are of no use for some days, if kept longer.

3. **Leaving the line on being relieved.**

(a) He will have an up-to-date diagram of the communications of his Battalion to hand over to the relieving Signal Officer.

(b) He will proceed round his Battalion Communications with the relieving Battalion Signal Officer.

(c) He will make certain that no personnel found by him for visual, power buzzer stations etc. leave before the incoming personnel have taken over. He should receive a message from each of these stations, from the incoming personnel to this effect.

APPX/  War Diary

S E C R E T.    Copy No. 23

## 102nd INFANTRY BRIGADE ORDER No. 236

Ref. Maps -
Sheets 27 & 28
1:40,000.                                         AUG. 26th, 1918.

1. The 34th Division (less Artillery) will be relieved by the 14th Division (less Artillery).

2. The 102nd Infantry Brigade will be relieved by the 41st Infantry Brigade.

3. Battalions on relief will proceed according to attached Table "A".

4. The 1 Officer and 16 O.R's 102nd Inf. Bde. in GREEN Line and the 1 Officer and 16 other ranks in the YELLOW Line will be relieved by the 42nd Infantry Brigade but will remain in their respective positions for 24 hours after relief and then proceed to join their Units at ROAD CAMP 27/F.25.c. d.

5. The 1/4th Bn. Cheshire Regt. will be relieved by the 29th Bn. D. L. I. on the morning of 27.8.18.

   The 1/1st Bn. Herefordshire Regt. will be relieved by the 18th Y. & L. on the morning of 27.8.18.

   The 1/7th Bn. Cheshire Regt. will be relieved by the 33rd London Regt. on the evening of 27.8.18.

6. All Battalions 102nd Infantry Brigade will detrain at LANCASTER Station 27/F.19.c.5.8. and proceed to Road Camp according to Table "A". Guides for each Battalion will be at LANCASTER Station.

7. Guides - Guides from 1/4th Bn. Cheshire Regt. will be at MISSION JUNCTION at 11.0 a.m. to meet 29th D.L.I. 1 Officer, in charge of guides, and 1 other ranks per battalion Headquarters and 2 other ranks per Company.

   Guides from 1/1st Bn. Herefordshire Regt. will be at KEMMEL BECQ SPUR, B.26.b.1.9. at 12 noon to meet the 18th Yorks & Lancs. 1 Officer, in charge of guides, and 1 O.R. per Battn. Headquarters and 2 O.R's per Coy.

   Guides from 1/7th Bn. Cheshire Regt. will be at TRIANGLE G.6.a.8.2. at 7.0 p.m. to meet the 33rd London Regt. 1 Officer, in charge of guides, 1 O.R. per Battalion Headquarters, and 2 O.R's per Company.

   Guides from the L. T. M. B. will be at TRIANGLE, G.6.a.8.2 to meet the 41st L. T. M. B. at 7.0 p.m. - 1 O. R. only.

8. Advance parties of the 41st Inf. Bde. will report at 102nd Brigade Headquarters at 8.0 a.m. and will be sent up to Battalions immediately on arrival.

9. All trench stores, maps, defence schemes, R.E. material and stores and Lewis Guns and Anti-aircraft posts will be handed over and receipts forwarded to Brigade Headquarters by 10.0 a.m. August 28th, 1918.

.. All movement ...

( 2 )

10. All movement East of the POPERINGHE - PROVEN road will be by platoons at 100 yards distance.
East of VLAMERTINGHE all movement will be by Sections at 100 yards distance.

11. Divisional Headquarters will remain at LA LOVIE pending further instructions.

12. Transport will move in accordance with attached Table "B".

13. Brigade Headquarters will close here on completion of relief and open at ROAD CAMP at the same hour.

14. O's. C. Battalions will report completion of relief by code word 'S P O T' by wire to Advanced Brigade Headquarters and arrival at ROAD CAMP to Headquarters there as soon as it opens.

15. All details at present with Wagon lines will join their respective Units by 9.30 a.m. 27.8.18.

16. Acknowledge.

A.B.Leake.
Capt.
a/BRIGADE MAJOR.
102nd INFANTRY BRIGADE.

Distribution -

Copy No. 1 G.O.C.
2 A/E.M.
3 Staff Captain.
4 Bde. Transport Officer.
5 O.C. 102 Bde. Signals.
6 1/4th Bn Cheshire Regt.
7 1/7th Bn Cheshire Regt.
8 1/1st Bn Hereford Regt.
9 102nd L.T.M.B.
10 No. 3 Coy. Train.
11 O.C. 102 Bde. Supply.
12 207th Field Co. R.E.
13 208th Field Co. R.E.
14 Sector Comdt. GREEN LINE.
15 Sector Comdt. YELLOW LINE.
16 34th Division.
17 44th Division.
18 101st Inf. Bde.
19 103rd Inf. Bde.
20 41st Inf. Bde.
21 12th Belgian Division.
22 Area Comdt. ST. JAN TER BIEZEN.

23 & 24 War Diary and File.

SECRET.

## 102nd INFANTRY BRIGADE ADMINISTRATIVE INSTRUCTIONS NO. 11.

To Accompany 102nd Brigade Order No. 226 - August 25th, 1918.

Ref. Map
Sheet No. 28,
1/40,000.

1. **SUPPLIES.**

   Supplies for consumption 26th will be refilled at ROAD CAMP tomorrow, after Train Coy have Refilled from Railhead. - Exact time can be ascertained by units at ROAD CAMP.

2. **BAGGAGE.**

   ½ a Lorry is at the disposal of each Battalion for extra baggage etc. Units will send a guide to CROSS ROADS - A.20.central at 9-55am to meet them. 1/1st Herefords and 1/4th Cheshires will have one and 1/7th Cheshires, Brigade Hqrs., and L.T.M.B. the other. The first named will load first.

3. **GUIDES ETC LEFT BEHIND TO HAND OVER TO INCOMING UNITS.**

   Those of the 1/4th Bn. Cheshire Regt. will travel on the 1/1st Bn. Hereford Regt. train at 4pm from KEMMELBECQ - B.28.b.1.9.
   Those of the 1/1st Bn. Hereford Regt. will travel on the 1/7th Bn. Cheshire Regt. train at 8pm from TRIANGLE - G.6.a.8.2.

4. **CLEANLINESS OF CAMP.**

   The usual certificate of cleanliness of Camp will be forwarded by last Runner before the Battalion moves.

5. **FIELD AMBULANCE.**

   The location of the 102nd Field Ambulance will be *Lister Camp W 23 a 3 8*

6. **LEAVE.**

   Leave Parties will proceed from MENDINGHEM as usual.

   Captain.
   Staff Captain.
   102nd Infantry Brigade.

25/8/18.

102nd Infantry Brigade Administrative Instructions No. 12.

To accompany 102nd Brigade Order No. 237 dated 27/8/18.

1. ENTRAINMENT.

One Officer from each Battalion and L.T.M.B. will report to an Officer of 102nd Brigade H.Q. at the R.T.Os. Office PROVEN at 7-30am. He will bring with him the exact Entraining Strength of his unit.

The accommodation in the train will probably be used to its full capacity. The Advance Officer from each unit will ascertain from Officer I/c Entraining how many trucks are allotted and the unit will be detailed off accordingly before any Entrainment commences.

2. 1/4th DETACHMENT PROCEEDING AT 6am.

This detachment of 250 all ranks will report to the Personnel Officer, R.T.O. MENDINGHEM at 5-45am for accommodation on the Personnel Train.

3. SUPPLIES.

The preserved rations refilled tonight will be carried in the Supply Wagons and consumed in the case of the Mounted Personnel on August 29th and in the case of the Dismounted Personnel proceeding by Rail on August 30th.

Rations for Dismounted Personnel for consumption on the 29th will be delivered by lorries at CORMETTE CAMP tomorrow.

4. BAGGAGE ETC.

One lorry per Battalion for the conveyance of Kits, Cooking material etc. will report at ROAD CAMP at 9am. These lorries must be loaded and ready to move off by 9-30am.

5. ADVANCE PARTIES.

One Officer and 2 O.R. per Battalion will proceed by these lorries as Advance Parties.

6. L.T.M.B.

One G.S. wagon and one G.S. Limber will report at Brigade H.Qrs. at 5-45am for the guns, baggage etc., of the L.T.M.B. where a guide will meet them. They will return to Brigade H.Q. immediately after loading.

The 4 Officers Kits - Mess Kit and mens Camp Kettles will be dumped in charge of one man at Brigade Hqrs., by 7am. This man will act as Advance Party for L.T.M.B.

7. SADDLE HORSES.

All Saddle Horses will proceed to CORMETTE CAMP in one journey. They will report at X Roads F.25.c.2.2. at 8-0am to the Brigade Signalling Officer and will march under his orders. Rations and Forage for consumption 29th August for this party will be put on the lorries.

NOTE.

Units will take over the same accommodation in CORMETTE Musketry Camp as they had during the recent visit in July.

Captain.
Staff Captain.
102nd Infantry Brigade.

27/8/18.

102nd Infantry Brigade Administrative Instructions No. 12.

To accompany 102nd Brigade Order No. 237 dated 27/8/18.

------------------------------------------

1. ENTRAINMENT.

    One Officer from each Battalion and L.T.M.B. will report to an Officer of 102nd Brigade H.Q. at the R.T.Os. Office PROVEN at 7-30am. He will bring with him the exact Entraining Strength of his unit.

    The accommodation in the train will probably be used to its full capacity. The Advance Officer from each unit will ascertain from Officer I/c Entraining how many trucks are allotted and the unit will be detailed off accordingly before any Entrainment commences.

2. 1/4th DETACHMENT PROCEEDING AT 6am.

    This detachment of 250 all ranks will report to the Personnel Officer, R.T.O. MENDINGHEM at 5-45am for accommodation on the Personnel Train.

3. SUPPLIES.

    The preserved rations refilled tonight will be carried in the Supply Wagons and consumed in the case of the Mounted Personnel on August 29th and in the case of the Dismounted Personnel proceeding by Rail on August 30th.

    Rations for Dismounted Personnel for consumption on the 29th will be delivered by lorries at CORMETTE CAMP tomorrow.

4. BAGGAGE ETC.

    One lorry per Battalion for the conveyance of Kits, Cooking material etc. will report at ROAD CAMP at 9am. These lorries must be loaded and ready to move off by 9-30am.

5. ADVANCE PARTIES.

    One Officer and 2 O.R. per Battalion will proceed by these lorries as Advance Parties.

6. L.T.M.B.

    One G.S. wagon and one G.S. Limber will report at Brigade H.Qrs. at 5-45am for the guns, baggage etc., of the L.T.M.B. where a guide will meet them. They will return to Brigade H.Q. immediately after loading.

    The 4 Officers Kits - Mess Kit and mens Camp Kettles will be dumped in charge of one man at Brigade Hqrs., by 7am. This man will act as Advance Party for L.T.M.B.

7. SADDLE HORSES.

    All Saddle Horses will proceed to CORMETTE CAMP in one journey. They will report at X Roads F.25.c.2.2. at 8-0am to the Brigade Signalling Officer and will march under his orders. Rations and Forage for consumption 29th August for this party will be put on the lorries.

    NOTE.

    Units will take over the same accommodation in CORMETTE Musketry Camp as they had during the recent visit in July.

27/8/18.

Captain.
Staff Captain.
102nd Infantry Brigade.

Table "A"   (To accompany 102nd Inf. Bde. Order No. 236)

| Date | No. | Unit | Relieved | | Times | Detraining | Destination |
|---|---|---|---|---|---|---|---|
| | | | By | At | | Station | |
| Aug. 27th | 1 | 1/4th Cheshire Rgt. | 29th D.L.I. | BROWN Line. | (a) 12 noon (b) 12.10 pm (c) 12.20 pm | LANCASTER STATION 27/F.19.c.5.8. | ROAD CAMP ST. JAN TER BIEZEN. |
| - do - | 2 | 1/1st Bn. Hereford Rgt. | 18th York & Lancs. | SIEGE CAMP. | (a) 4.0 p.m. (b) 4.10 p.m. (c) 4.20 p.m. | - do - | - do - |
| - do - | 3 | 1/7th Bn. Cheshire Regt. | 55rd London Regt. | BRAKE CAMP. | (a) 8.0 p.m. (b) 8.10 p.m. (c) 8.20 p.m. | - do - | - do - |
| - do - | 4 | 102nd L.T.M.B. | 41st L.T.M.B. | -do- | 8.0 p.m. | - do - | - do - |
| - do - | 5 | 102nd Inf. Bde. Hd. Qrs. | 41st Inf. Bde. Hd. Qrs. | BRAKE CAMP. | - | - | - do - |

Notes -
1. There will be three trains for each Battalion - one of 10 trucks and two of 9. Each truck to hold 20 to 25.
2. Units will be at Entraining Station 20 minutes before scheduled hour of departure.
3. Battalions will detail an Officer to go in advance and superintend entraining of his Battalion.

TABLE "D" (To accompany 102 Inf. Bde. Order No. 235)

Starting Point .. Cross Roads 28/A.23.a.9.0.

| Date | No. | UNIT | Relieved By | To be clear of Starting Point by | Route | Destination |
|---|---|---|---|---|---|---|
| Aug. 27th | 1 | 1/4th Battn. Cheshire Regt. | 29th D.L.I. | 11.0 a.m. | A.23.a.4.0. | ROAD CAMP |
| Aug. 27th | 2 | 1/1st Battn. Herefordshire Regt. | 18th York & Lancs. | 11.30 am | A.3.c.1.9. Switch Road | ST. JAN |
| Aug. 27th | 3 | 1/7th Battn. Cheshire Regt. | 33rd London Regt. | 12.0 noon | N. of POPERINGHE - ST. JAN TER BIEZEN | TER BIEZEN |

Notes - Transports will march under Battalion Transport Officers - Interval of 25X between each set of 6 vehicles will be maintained. Mess carts may proceed independently.

II. Corps G.S.9

27th August, 1917.

Fifth Army.
―――――――

I send you herewith for the information of the Army Commander, copy of a report by the G.O.C., 74th Infantry Brigade on the operations which were carried out on the 10th/11th August.

(sd) C.W. Jacob

Lieutenant-General,
Commanding II Corps.

APP 1F

War Diary

TO BE ACKNOWLEDGED         **SECRET.**                    Copy No. 16
BY BEARER

102nd INFANTRY BRIGADE ORDER No. 237.

Ref. Maps -
Sheet 27 1/40,000
HAZEBROUCK 5a 1/100,000                                   Aug. 27th 1918

102 Brigade    1. The 102nd Brigade Group as per margin, will move to
"A" Coy. M.G.     CORNETTE CAMP on 28th and 29th August.
Battalion.     (a) Dismounted personnel will proceed by rail on August 28th
Detachment         entraining at PROVEN. Moves to the entraining Station
102 Field          will be carried out in accordance with Table "A" attached.
Ambulance.     (b) Mounted personnel and Transport will proceed by March
                   Route on August 28th and 29th under the orders of O.C.
                   No. 3 Coy. Train, in accordance with Table "B" attached,
                   staying one night at LEDERZEELE.

               2. The detachment of the 102nd Field Ambulance will proceed
                  independently on the 28th August under orders to be issued
                  by the A.D.M.S. and come under the orders of O.C. No. 3 Coy.
                  Train at LEDERZEELE, reporting to him on arrival at Area
                  Commandant's office. The same applies to the mounted
                  personnel of "A" Coy., 34th Bn. M.G.C.

               3.   Administrative instructions are being issued by the
                    Staff Captain.

               4.   Distances on the march will be maintained as laid down
                    in this office T.S. 67/1 dated July 2nd 1918.

               5.   Dress will be full marching order. S.D. caps will be
                    worn. Steel helmets will be carried on the back of the
                    pack affixed to the two braces.

               6.   102nd Brigade Headquarters will close at ROAD CAMP
                    at 9.0 a.m. and re-open on arrival at CORNETTE CAMP.

                                                   _J.M.M Carlisle_
                    102 B.H.Q.                              Captain.
                                                    A/ BRIGADE MAJOR.
        Issued at         p.m.               102nd INFANTRY BRIGADE.

               Distribution -
                    Copy No. 1   G.O.C.
                           2     Brigade Major.
                           3     Staff Captain.
                           4     1/4th Bn Cheshire Regt.
                           5     1/7th Bn Cheshire Regt.
                           6     1/1st Bn Hereford Regt.
                           7     34th M. G. Battn.
                           8     102nd L.T.M.B.
                           9     No. 3 Coy. Train.
                          10     102nd Bde. Supply Officer.
                          11     Bde. Transport Officer.
                          12     102nd Field Ambulance.
                          13     34th Division.
                          14     A.D.M.S., 34th Div.
                          15     R.T.O. PROVEN.
                          16     War Diary
                                        &
                          17         File.

TO BE ACKNOWLEDGED      S E C R E T.               Copy No...
BY BEARER.

## 102nd INFANTRY BRIGADE ORDER No. 237.

Ref. Maps -
Sheet 27 1/40,000
HAZEBROUCK 5a 1/100,000                                    Aug. 27th 1918.

102 Brigade    1. The 102nd Brigade Group as per margin, will move to
"A" Coy. M.G.      CORMETTE CAMP on 28th and 29th August.
Battalion.      (a) Dismounted personnel will proceed by rail on August 28th
Detachment           entraining at PROVEN. Moves to the entraining Station
102 Field             will be carried out in accordance with Table "A" attached.
Ambulance.    (b) Mounted personnel and Transport will proceed by March
                  Route on August 28th and 29th under the orders of O.C.
                  No. 3 Coy. Train, in accordance with Table "B" attached,
                  staging one night at LEDERZEELE.

2. The detachment of the 102nd Field Ambulance will proceed
independently on the 28th August under orders to be issued
by the A.D.M.S. and come under the orders of O.C. No. 3 Coy.
Train at LEDERZEELE, reporting to him on arrival at Area
Commandant's office. The same applies to the mounted
personnel of "A" Coy., 34th Bn. M.G.C.

3.      Administrative instructions are being issued by the
Staff Captain.

4.      Distances on the march will be maintained as laid down
in this office T.S. 67/1 dated July 2nd 1918.

5.      Dress will be full marching order. S.D. caps will be
worn. Steel helmets will be carried on the back of the
pack affixed to the two braces.

6.      102nd Brigade Headquarters will close at ROAD CAMP
at 9.0 a.m. and re-open on arrival at CORMETTE CAMP.

                                           *J.M.M. Carlisle*   Captain.
     102 B.H.Q.                                      A/ BRIGADE MAJOR.
   Issued at        p.m.                 102nd INFANTRY BRIGADE.

         Distribution -
                Copy No. 1   G.O.C.
                        2   Brigade Major.
                        3   Staff Captain.
                        4   1/4th Bn Cheshire Regt.
                        5   1/7th Bn Cheshire Regt.
                        6   1/1st Bn Hereford Regt.
                        7   34th M.G. Battn.
                        8   102nd L.T.M.B.
                        9   No. 3 Coy. Train.
                       10   102nd Bde. Supply Officer.
                       11   Bde. Transport Officer.
                       12   102nd Field Ambulance.
                       13   34th Division.
                       14   A.D.M.S., 34th Div.
                       15   R.T.O. PROVEN.
                       16   War Diary
                               &
                       17     File.

March Table "A" - To accompany Bde. Order No. 237

| Serial No. | Date | UNIT | From | To | Starting Point | Time | Route | Time of departure of trains. |
|---|---|---|---|---|---|---|---|---|
| 1. | 28.8.18 | 250 All ranks 1/4th Ches. Rgt. | ROAD CAMP | PROVEN STATION. | F.25.c.2.2. | 4.45 a.m. | Road running North through F.25.c. to Cross Roads in E.12.d. thence to PROVEN. | 6.0 a.m. |
| 2. | - do - | 1/4th Cheshire Regt. (less 250 All ranks). | - do - | - do - | - do - | 6.15 a.m. | - do - | 8.45 a.m. |
| 3. | - do - | 1/7th Cheshire Regt. | - do - | - do - | - do - | 6.19 a.m. | - do - | - do - |
| 4. | - do - | 1/1st Hereford Regt. | - do - | - do - | - do - | 6.28 a.m. | - do - | - do - |
| 5. | - do - | 102nd Bde. Headquarters & 102nd L.T.M.B. | - do - | - do - | - do - | 6.38 a.m. 6.40 a.m. | - do - | - do - |
| 6. | - do - | "A" Coy. 34th M.G. Battn. | A.30.central. | - do - | To proceed as ordered by O.C. M.G. Coy. | | | 8.45 a.m. |

March Table "A" - To accompany Bde. Order No. 237

| Serial No. | Date | UNIT | From | To | Starting Point | Time | Route | Time of departure of trains. |
|---|---|---|---|---|---|---|---|---|
| 1. | 28.8.18 | 250 All ranks 1/4th Ches. Rgt. | ROAD CAMP | PROVEN STATION. | F.25.c.2.2. | 4.45 a.m. | Road running North through F.25.c. to Cross Roads in E.12.d. thence to PROVEN. | 6.0 a.m. |
| 2. | - do - | 1/4th Cheshire Regt. (less 250 All ranks). | - do - | - do - | - do - | 6.15 a.m. | - do - | 8.45 a.m. |
| 3. | - do - | 1/7th Cheshire Regt. | - do - | - do - | - do - | 6.19 a.m. | - do - | - do - |
| 4. | - do - | 1/1st Hereford Regt. | - do - | - do - | - do - | 6.28 a.m. | - do - | - do - |
| 5. | - do - | 102nd Bde. Headquarters & 102nd L.T.M.B. | - do - | - do - | - do - | 6.38 a.m. 6.40 a.m. | - do - | - do - |
| 6. | - do - | "A" Coy. 34th M.G. Battn. | A.30.central. | do. | To proceed as ordered by O.C. M.G. Coy. | | | 8.45 a.m. |

March Table "B" — To accompany 102nd Inf. Bde. Order No. 237.

| Serial No. | Date | Unit | From | To | Starting Point | Time | Route | REMARKS |
|---|---|---|---|---|---|---|---|---|
| 1. | 29.8.18 | Transport 102nd Bde. Hd. Qrs. & 102nd L.T.M.B. | ROAD CAMP. | LEDERZEELE. | Cross Roads in E.30.c.4.5. | 10.2 a.m. | HOUTKERQUE WERZEELE WORMHOUDT ZEGGERS-CAPPEL | |
| 2. | -do- | T'port 1/4th Cheshire Regt. | -do- | -do- | -do- | 10.5 a.m. | -do- | |
| 3. | -do- | T'port 1/7th Cheshire Regt. | -do- | -do- | -do- | 10.10 a.m. | -do- | |
| 4. | -do- | T'port 1/1st Hereford Regt. | -do- | -do- | -do- | 10.15 a.m. | -do- | |
| 5. | -do- | No. 3 Coy. Train | F.19.d. central. | -do- | -do- | 10.20 a.m. | -do- | Not to pass Starting Point till 1/1st Bn. Hereford Regt. are clear. |
| 6. | -do- | T'port "A" Co. 34th M.G. Battn. | 28/A.30.central | -do- | -do- | -do- | -do- | To march independently under orders of O.C. 34th M.G. Bn. |
| 7. | -do- | 102nd Fld. Amb. | LISTER CAMP. | CORBETTE. | -do- | -do- | -do- | Under orders of A.D.M.S. |
| | 29.8.18 | 102 Bde. Group. | LEDERZEELE. | CORBETTE. | | | | To proceed under orders of O.C. No. 3 Coy. Train. |

March Table "B" — To accompany 102nd Inf. Bde. Order No. 237.

| Serial | Date | Unit | From | To | Starting Point | Time | Route | REMARKS. |
|---|---|---|---|---|---|---|---|---|
| 1. | 28.8.18 | Transport 102nd Bde. Hd. Qrs. & 102nd L.T.M.B. | ROAD CAMP. | LEDERZEELE. | Cross Roads in E.30.c.4.5. | 10.2 a.m | | |
| 2. | -do- | T'port 1/4th Cheshire Regt. | -do- | -do- | -do- | 10.5 a.m. | -do- | |
| 3. | -do- | T'port 1/7th Cheshire Regt. | -do- | -do- | -do- | 10.10 a.m. | -do- | |
| 4. | -do- | T'port 1/1st Hereford Regt. | -do- | -do- | -do- | 10.15 a.m. | -do- | |
| 5. | -do- | No. 3 Coy. Train | F.19.d. central. | -do- | -do- | 10.20 a.m. | -do- | Not to pass Starting Point till 1/1st Bn. Hereford Regt. are clear. |
| 6. | -do- | T'port "A" Co. 34th M.G. Battn. | 28/A.30.central | -do- | | | -do- | To march independently under orders of O.C. 34th M.G. Bn. |
| 7. | -do- | 102nd Fld. Amb. | LISTER CAMP. | -do- | | | -do- | Under orders of A.D.M.S. |
| | 29.8.18 | 102 Bde. Group. | LEDERZEELE. | CORNETTE. | | | | To proceed under orders of O.C. No. 3 Coy. Train. |

Table "D".  ENTRAINING TABLE to accompany 102nd Inf. Bde. Order No. 232 (Addendum).

Entraining Station .. LE PLESSIS BELLEVILLE.

| Ser. No. | Date | Unit | Time of arrival at entraining station. | Time of departure of train. | Detraining station. | Remarks |
|---|---|---|---|---|---|---|
| 1. | 9.4.18 | Transport, 102nd Inf. Bde.H.Q. & Signal Section. "F" Coy. N.G. Battn. | 2.0 a.m. | 3.9 a.m. | Not yet known. | |
| 2. | -do- | 102nd Inf. Bde. Hd. Qrs. Bde. Signal Section. 22nd L.T.M. Battery. "F" Coy. M.G. Battn. 120 O.R. 1/7th Ches. Regt. (unloading party) Advance parties all units. | 4.30 a.m. | 6.9 a.m. | -do- | |
| 3. | -do- | T'port, 1/4th Bn. Ches. Regt. | 6.0 a.m. | 10.9 a.m. | -do- | |
| 4. | -do- | 1/4th Bn. Cheshire Regt. | 8.30 a.m. | 10.9 a.m. | -do- | |
| 5. | -do- | 1/7th Bn. Cheshire Regt. | 10 a.m. | 2.9 p.m. | -do- | |
| 6. | -do- | 1/7th Bn. Ches. Regt. (less unloading party.) | 12.50 p.m. | 2.9 p.m. | -do- | |
| 7. | -do- | T'port, 1/1st Hereford Regt. | 2.0 p.m. | 6.9 p.m. | -do- | |
| 8. | -do- | 1/1st Bn. Hereford Regt. (less loading party) | 4.30 p.m. | 6.9 p.m. | -do- | |
| 9. | -do- | T'port, No. 3 Coy. Train T'port, 208th Field Co.R.E. | 6.0 p.m. | 10.9 p.m. | -do- | |
| 10. | -do- | No. 5 Coy. Train. 208th Field Co. R.E. loading party 1/1st Bn. Herefordshire Regt. | 8.30 p.m. | 10.9 p.m. | -do- | |

www.ingramcontent.com/pod-product-compliance
Lightning Source LLC
Chambersburg PA
CBHW081543160426
43191CB00011B/1827